AFFILIATE MARKETING MADE EASY

BEGINNER'S GUIDE

UNLOCK THE SECRETS OF AFFILIATE MARKETING AND MASTER THE ART OF MAKING MONEY ONLINE

Jack S. Hood

All rights reserved

No part of this work may be reproduced, incorporated into a computer system, or transmitted in any form or by any means (electronic, mechanical, photocopying, recording or otherwise) without the prior written permission of the copyright holders. Infringement of such rights may constitute an intellectual property crime.

Disclaimer clause.
My lawyer insists that I communicate...
Please note that the information contained in this document is for educational and entertainment purposes only.

Every effort has been made to present accurate, up-to-date and reliable information. No warranty of any kind is stated or implied. Readers acknowledge that the author is not engaged in rendering legal, financial, or professional advice.

The contents of this book have been derived from various sources. Consult a licensed professional before attempting any technique described in this book. By reading this document, you agree that under no circumstances is the author liable for any loss, direct or indirect, that may be incurred as a result of the use of the information contained herein, including, but not limited to errors, omissions, or inaccuracies.

Under no circumstances shall the publisher, or the author, be held liable or legally responsible for any damages, repairs, or monetary losses due to the information contained in this book. Directly or indirectly.

No part of this book may be reproduced or stored in a retrieval system or transmitted in any form or by any means, electronic, photocopying, recording or otherwise, without the express permission of the author.

Part 1. Fundamentals 4
What is Affiliate Marketing. No nonsense 4
Passive Income 7
Business idea 9
The 8 must-know features of affiliate marketing 10
Pros and cons of affiliate marketing 18
The 4 key players in affiliate marketing 21
Part 2. Market niches 34
What is a niche market and how to choose one? 34
The 5 key aspects to consider when choosing a niche market 35
Market niche. Demand and competitiveness 37
250 market niches 45
Part 3. Criteria for choosing affiliate programs 57
How to Choose the Right Affiliate Program: 7 Keys to Success 57
The right price 62
Part 4. Web and Traffic 65
How to create a good, beautiful and cheap affiliate website 65
The secret: 2 X 10 77
How to drive traffic to your affiliate links 77
How to attract traffic to your affiliate links The 15 foolproof methods to get 15,000 free visits in 15 days 79
Blogs that fail. The three most frequent and stupid mistakes they make. How to avoid them 90
Part 5. Best affiliate programs for beginners 92
Discover the 20 best affiliate programs for beginners who want to go from €0 to €10,000 per month 92
Part 6. Examples of affiliate websites 114
25 best affiliate marketing websites. Number 15 will amaze you. Get inspired! 114
25 turnover estimates. The results will fill you with optimism 138
How to do affiliate marketing on social networks 145
Part 7. The Road 147
The treasure trail to a monthly turnover of 10,000 €. Step by step guide. Checklist 147
Hi, I'm Jack 151

Part 1. Fundamentals

What is Affiliate Marketing. No nonsense

*Affiliate marketing has enabled Alex Goldberg and Healy Jones to go from $0 to $20,000 monthly turnover with their review website **FinvsFin.com**, in less than 6 months and with minimal investment.*

Affiliate marketing is a business model that makes it easy to become **financially independent,** bye bye boss, with little or no investment, by recommending products and earning a commission from the merchant.

Case Study

The founding team of **choosewheels.com** has transformed their love for electric and eco-friendly transportation into a "sustainable" business model thanks to affiliate marketing.

They provide quality and useful content of the type:
- 5 best hoverboards / self-balancing scooters
- Top 10 best electric motorcycles in 2020
- The 7 best Segway boards of 2020
- Segway i2 vs. Segway x2: a detailed comparison
- How much does it cost to charge an electric car?

Monetize with **Amazon's** affiliate program. **Amazon Associates.** This e-commerce empire pays them a commission for each sale obtained from the traffic referred from **choosewheels.com** to their website.

The **three** key **aspects** of affiliate marketing are:
1- It is a **model of digital entrepreneurship.**
2- Allows the affiliate to obtain a **commission.** An economic income.
3- The result of **promoting** the merchant's products, through sales or the performance of a specific action, such as registering on the merchant's website.

Key idea
Affiliate marketing is a branch of online marketing that is based on the achievement of certain results or actions.

Affiliates (companies, websites,...) are responsible for advertising merchants (stores, advertisers, service providers) by publishing their advertisements or promotions.

The affiliate gets a percentage of each sale that occurs and has been promoted by the affiliate. For companies that sponsor affiliate programs, this pay-per-success model allows them to promote their brand and products and increase sales, incurring costs only when sales occur.

Affiliate Marketing is a **WIN-WIN model.** Everybody wins:
   A- Companies incur advertising **expenses** only if they **sell**.
   B- Affiliates earn commissions with a **minimum investment**, without the need to create a product.

Case Study
www.younghouselove.com is a successful home decorating and DIY blog created by **John** and **Sherry,** home decorating, DIY and renovation enthusiasts.

Monthly web traffic: **400,000** visits. **They monetize** their website as affiliates of the following retailers:
- amazon.com
- homedepot.com
- worldmarket.com
- target.com
- serenaandlily.com
- wayfair.com.

Example of **Sherry** and **John's** publications on their website:
- How to store everything in a small kitchen
- How to paint an abstract and colorful mural
- How to clean a dirty second hand carpet
- Necessary tools and tips for self-installing an Ikea kitchen

John and **Sherry** publish decorating ideas and tips. They recount their home renovation and decorating experiences, recounting the nearly **3,000** projects and decorating ideas they have undertaken to give their homes a new life.

They promote products they have used in the works and decorative items.

Time to act

Do you like decorating... Yes, read the whole guide and **act now!** The time is now!

You can create your own decoration and renovation blog, like Sherry and John. Monetize with Amazon and Lerroy Merlin affiliate programs.

Read on to find out how much you will earn (commission rate, where to sign up, how to have a blog for less than 15€...).

This book is the manual you need to start your **digital empire** based on Affiliate Marketing and enjoy the life you deserve, whether you live in Madrid, Teruel, Chiapas or Buffalo (South Dakota, considered the poorest county in the USA).

$ $ $ $ $

Passive Income

Affiliate marketing is a "Passive Income Source".

You work hard today. You earn income tomorrow, next week, next month, the next few months and, by updating the content, you will receive juicy income for years to come.

Comparison between active and passive income:

Active income:
This is the traditional way of **actively and regularly earning an income through** paid professional performance.
You know, the typical exchange of working hours for a salary. It's the usual 9:00 a.m. to 5:00 p.m. job of a lifetime.

Passive income:
Affiliate marketing as a source of passive income consists of spending a number of hours to **create a "digital property** that produces **passive income"**, i.e. a **website** with **useful content**, promoting products, providing tips, ideas, generating traffic to the merchant's website, conversions and affiliate commissions.

This is what Jhon & Sherry achieve with their blog younghouselove.com, publishing valuable and useful content for their audience. Of course, they do it when they want to, when they can or when they feel like it.

Internet does the rest, you know, positioning, visits, targeted traffic to merchants' websites, sales and commissions. 7 days a week and 24 hours a day.

All without Sherry and John having to be constantly in front of the laptop.

*Thanks to **passive income** Jhon and Sherry can be sipping mojitos by their pool in Florida, in Hawaii or in Bombay.*

*Its digital property, known as **younghouselove.com**, together with its partners (Amazon, Home Depot, Target...) generates thousands of $$$$$.*

Affiliate marketing is a passive income generator, as an affiliate you create your digital property. You decide:
- Which products to promote.
- What content you create.
- Generate traffic to your blog.
- Create a community.
- Refer visits to the merchant's website.
- Purchasing (conversion).
- Earn commissions (passive income).

At the beginning, at start-up you have to dedicate time and effort, but once your system, your **digital property, is** launched, the dedication required is minimal, just maintenance and updating.

Key idea

This **digital property** produces benefits **24 hours a day, 7 days a week**, generating income, without the need to fall into "presenteeism" and having to work anchored to the computer from 8:00 to 17:00.

In addition, as your turnover increases, you can outsource tasks to virtual collaborators and dedicate your time to new projects that increase your sources of passive income.

More digital properties, more niches, more revenue streams.

Isn't it wonderful? In affiliate marketing, promotional content generated in the past, produces income in the future, automatically. This is the magic of passive income.

Affiliate marketing is a money making machine

$ $ $ $ $

Business idea

Do you like the world of health and beauty? Do you follow it? How would you like to enjoy creating a website, share useful and interesting content and monetize with **promofarma.com**'s affiliate program?

Promofarma is a pharmaceutical marketplace with more than 45,000 products in its catalog and more than 500 pharmacies.

Commissions. With the **promofarma** affiliation program you can earn the following **income:**
- Standard commission. 0 - 100 monthly sales:
    - New customer: **8.5%** - Repeat customer: **5%**.
- Commission from 101 monthly sales:
    - New customer: **12%** - Repeat customer: **8.00**
- Commission for coupon websites: Linear commission of **5%**.

You can get up to 12% commission on sales from traffic sent from your website, from your affiliate links, to promofarma.com.

Create your online site in the health sector, write articles of type:
- Top 9 Anti-Dandruff Shampoos: Which one is best suited to your hair type?
- The 7 best organic and natural sunscreens
- The 5 best solid and ecological shampoos
- The 7 benefits of vitamin D from sunlight
- The 5 safest approved face masks for your daughters
- The TOP 5 of the best collagens
- The 4 best organic aloe vera brands to nourish your skin
- The 7 best digital thermometers for forehead or pistol thermometers
- The 9 best wrist blood pressure monitors.

$ $ $ $ $

The 8 must-know features of affiliate marketing

The 8 characteristics that distinguish affiliate marketing and that you should know are:

First. Obtain a return without having to create a product.

Affiliate marketing is a type of performance-based marketing. The affiliate promotes a product or a service of a merchant, gets the commission only if the sale occurs.

In the following chart we see the percentages paid by **Amazon Associates** to its affiliates for each sale:

Product categories	Revenues for standard commissions
Amazon Fashion Clothing, shoes, jewelry, watches, luggage, Amazon private label fashion (women's, men's, children's)	10 %
Handmade	10 %
Home Furniture, do-it-yourself, home, kitchen and dining, patio, lawn and garden, power and hand tools	7 %
Consumables Beer, wine and spirits, food, baby pet products, beauty, health and personal care, personal care appliances, stationery and office supplies	6 %
Digital & media Books, ebooks for Kindle, music, DVD and Blu-ray, digital video games, software, digital software, digital music,	6 %

digital video	
Hobbies and Car Outdoor leisure, toys and games, sports and fitness, musical instruments, cars and motorcycles, business and industry products	6 %
Amazon Devices Fire TV, Kindle & Echo devices and accessories	3 %
Electronics and IT Computers, electronics, photography, major household appliances, home entertainment, smartphones and mobile telephony, video games	3 %
Video game consoles	1 %
Other categories (except gift vouchers)	3 %
Prime Wardrobe purchases, gift certificates	0 %

Source: https://affiliate-program.amazon.com

The theme works as follows: we send traffic to Amazon's website. If there are no sales **Amazon** does not pay, however, if the transaction occurs within 24 hours after we send the user from our website to the Marketplace (cookie duration period), Amazon will pay us the percentage that corresponds depending on the category of the product sold, for example, if it is an article of...

- Jewelry: 10%.
- Amazon fashion: 10% off
- Furniture: 7%.
- Pets: 6%.
- Toys for children: 6%.

Second. Types of retribution in affiliate marketing

There are different types of retribution in affiliate marketing, the main ones are:

- **Commission. Credit for success**

This is the most **common** payout in affiliate marketing. The affiliate promotes the products of a third party, the merchant. When a sale is made on the merchant's website, the affiliate receives the agreed commission. In this case, the affiliate is a commission agent.

I sell - You collect. I don't sell - You don't get paid.
It's as simple as that

More than 90% of affiliate marketing programs follow this scheme.

- Promote my products
Make him sell and you get your commission ...
Fdo. The Merchants

It is a **performance-based**, **results-driven** membership program model.

- **Cost per Click. CPC**

The affiliate is paid for each click on their website, blog or social networks.
In this case it is not necessary that the sale takes place, only the interaction. It is a pay-for-performance program.

- **Cost per share. CPA**

The affiliate gets paid when the user performs the action on the merchant's landing page, for example:
- When a user registers
- Fill out a form
- Request a quote
- Sign up for a newsletter
- Provide your mobile number
- Delivers other information

In other words, when the user performs the agreed action, the affiliate is paid.

Examples

Let's look at several **scenarios:**
- **BBVA** pays its affiliates 35 € for each registration and opening of an account in BBVA online.
  For example, an affiliate who promotes through his blog: bestfinancialproducts.com, BBVA's online account, preaching its virtues, benefits and advantages, will obtain 35 € for each interested registration.
- **Younited Credit.** 35 per enrollment for a valid lead fee of €35 per enrollment requesting a loan between €1,000 and €40,000.
- **Raisin.** Savings products platform, pays 60€ to its affiliates for each completed form.

Note: These amounts may vary because they are those in effect at the time of publishing this book. The important thing is that you keep the idea and the possibilities that affiliate marketing offers to generate income.

Third. Traffic. Generate and send

The successful affiliate is a **traffic generator and manager:**
- **Get** visitors to your blog.
- It refers, through its affiliate links, traffic to the merchant's website.

The successful affiliate attracts and sends traffic to the merchant's website.

A percentage of that traffic will translate into sales (this is the conversion rate) and provide commissions to the affiliate.

There are several ways to **generate traffic** in affiliate marketing, several channels in which to advertise our valuable content and get visitors:

1.- By the "Type of Traffic" that we can obtain depending on the channel of origin.

The traffic, the visits, can come from different sources. There are countless channels in which to publish and disseminate valuable and unique content. The main ones are:

- Post published on your blog with relevant information for the community that follows you, is what we call Content Marketing or Inbound Marketing.
- Videos on YouTube
- Live Webinars
- Social networks
- Email marketing
- Messaging platform such as whatsapp or telegram
- Affiliation links contained in an eBook, in a PDF, in a power point presentation(...)
- Maybe from a podcast...

We will dedicate a specific chapter to go deeper into this topic (How to get traffic to your affiliate links. 15 methods to get free visits)

Depending on the "Cost of Acquisition" the traffic can be:
❏ **Free of charge. Organic. SEO**

Users find your content through search engines or go directly to your blog, because they know you and type your name directly in the browser.

Getting organic traffic requires time and knowledge of SEO techniques. It does not happen overnight.

❏ **Paid. SEM**

The affiliate buys traffic, bets on accelerating its acquisition through investment in advertising. It gets traffic quickly, it acquires it.

In this case, the digital entrepreneur invests money by advertising on social networks (Facebook, Instagram, YouTube...) or search engines (Google Adwords).

Advertising will accelerate the achievement of your affiliate marketing goals.

Key idea
When you choose to buy traffic, for example on social networks (Facebook, Instagram, Twitter...) the results are immediate.

Fourth. Create valuable and unique content

The successful affiliate is a constant generator of **valuable** and **unique content** that he shares on his website.

Fifth. Founding a community

The successful affiliate **creates a community** of followers, of faithful apostles, of users, of believers who gravitate around the content of the niche and the products they promote.

> **For example,** you can create and lead communities .... :)
> - www.I-loveHarleyDavidson.com
> - www.Mykingdomforanelectricbike.com
> - www.runningwithoutborders.com

The more numerous, powerful and involved the community around your blog and the larger the list of newsletter subscribers, followers on social networks (Youtube, Facebook, Instagram) or any other platform on which you operate your affiliate marketing, the greater your economic results will be.

Powerful community. Growing bank account :)

Does it mean that if I don't have a community of followers I can't do affiliate marketing? No. It means that you have to plan from the first day you start in the affiliate marketing industry, what content you should create that is perceived to be quality, unique, relevant, capable of gaining followers and forging a community of believers.

Remember. Do it from Day 1. Minute 1

Want to speed up the process? Buy traffic. Invest a handful of euros in advertising on social networks (Facebook, Instagram...). Boost the creation of your community. Turn a few coins on Facebook into contacts (email addresses) to increase the list of subscribers to your newsletter and do email marketing.

Creating a community is a matter of:
1. **Effort and time.** You create valuable and relevant content. You seek, by applying SEO techniques, to appear in the first positions in Google.
2. **Money.** You buy traffic by investing in advertising
3. **Combine both options.** You create unique content and also invest in advertising on social networks.

Success stories
Online communities created and monetized through Affiliate Marketing:
- **aboutwheels.net**
  Guides, analysis and recommendations on everything related to sustainable urban mobility.
- **hacercercervezaartesanal.com**
  Everything related to the world of craft beer. Equipment, kits, ingredients and recipes to brew craft beer.
- **pasiondelmusico.com**
  Blog to help you choose, with analysis and comparisons, different musical instruments. Ukuleles, guitars, mics, music bars...

Sixth. Inexpensive entrepreneurship. Low cost
Affiliate marketing is a type of digital entrepreneurship that requires little investment, you can start your affiliate empire with a blog for **less than 15€.** In this book you will learn how.

There are even affiliate products that you can promote and get commissions without having a website. 0€ investment.

Seventh. Scalable
The Affiliate Marketing business is scalable, you don't need to create products, you only need to have an infrastructure and methodology to promote the products.

Create your first niche blog, promote products, fine tune the system and, when everything works, replicate, create another blog, attack another niche, succeed again..., outsource tasks (externalize), and so on and on and on and on....

Key idea
Affiliate marketing is a digital business model that allows you to go from zero € to a million € or the amount you want to get, with little investment and scalable. Take advantage of it

Eighth. Lone wolf or pack

Affiliate marketing is a type of venture that you can undertake alone or in a team.

Proposal
Start alone and as you increase turnover, build a team, delegate functions, outsource:
- Writing content
- Manage the web (Webmaster), supervise the proper functioning of your Blog or blogs...
- Positioning content (SEO expert), to optimize and appear first page in Google

$ $ $ $ $

Pros and cons of affiliate marketing

Let's look at the good and the not so good of affiliate marketing. The heads and tails, the yin and the yang.

Pros. Aspects in favor. We highlight the following benefits of affiliate marketing:
- **Minimal investment.** This is an inexpensive form of digital entrepreneurship.
  You can start without having to invest anything, promoting products from affiliate programs that do not require a website, among your contacts in social networks.
  It requires a minimal investment, within the reach of anyone.
  It is a business based on talent, not financial muscle.
- **Fast.** You don't need to create products to sell, just recommend and send traffic to the merchant's website through your affiliate links.
- **No headaches.** Customer service is provided by the merchant, not the affiliate.
- It's a **passive income** generator. You sow once (create relevant and unique content, please) and you get harvests over a long period of time.
- **Income potential.** You can earn as much income as you want, it all depends on how much effort you are willing to put in.

Cons. Disadvantages. The disadvantages or dangers to take into account are:
- **Customer misappropriation.** Users' contact details end up in the possession of the merchant, not the affiliate who has directed traffic to your site.

Usurpation occurs when the affiliate attracts traffic to its blog, redirects it to the merchant's site, there the sale occurs, the merchant captures the customer's data and the relationship continues only between merchant and customer, without paying commissions to the affiliate ever again.

Antidote: create your own subscriber list
The best vaccine to avoid this situation is to create your own list of subscribers. Capture the email addresses of your users to be able to do email marketing. Offer promotions, give away free gifts, for example "download the free ebook..." in exchange for the email address.

With your list of subscribers you can contact whenever you want, at the click of a button... SEND..., you keep in touch, you send new valuable content "wisely impregnated" with your affiliate links...

- **Falling into fraudulent affiliate programs**. You must be careful when choosing an affiliation program. Do your research to avoid falling into fraudulent networks, sometimes the Internet is the territory of pirates who, under cover of anonymity, take advantage of clueless people to steal their time (effort without return) and, in the worst case, their money.

Key idea
Never sign up for an affiliate program that asks for money when you sign up. It is probably a scam.

In many cases behind this request there is a pyramid scheme, or criminals who want to have access to your bank details and make your hard-earned money disappear.

Antidote. Collaborate only with programs and networks with excellent reputations, such as **Amazon Associates, Booking, Aliexpress, Fiverr, Udemy, BBVA...**

There are hundreds and hundreds of affiliate programs managed by serious, solvent and transparent companies. Don't complicate your life. Don't waste time and money. **Be "sapiens".**
Survival idea...

Run away from chimeras. Don't look for mythical affiliate programs with **fantastic** conditions.

It is likely that behind that **"Nirvana"** of potential earnings, there is a gang of crooks trying to take advantage of your work and, in the worst case, seeking to access your card data and rob you blind.

I insist. You have at your fingertips a large number of reliable affiliate programs, sponsored by reputable companies, which pay what is agreed and at the agreed time. **Don't complicate your life.**

Throughout this manual you will learn about dozens of trusted and reliable affiliate marketing programs.

$ $ $ $ $

The 4 key players in affiliate marketing

The **four key players** in affiliate marketing are:
1.- Merchant
2.- Affiliate
3.-Customer
4.- Marketing networks

Let's analyze each of them

1.- Merchant

The merchant sells the product or service to the user and pays the agreed commission to the affiliate.

There are different types of merchants in affiliate marketing:
- A. Brand
- B. Product creator
- C. Seller, often a marketplace

A.- Brand:

In this case, it is the organization itself, which owns the brand, that creates and manages the affiliate marketing program. This is the case of **NIKE**.

Example. NIKE

NIKE is an American multinational company engaged in the design, development, manufacture and marketing of sports equipment: balls, footwear, apparel, equipment, accessories and other sporting goods.

- 2020 Revenues: US$37**.4 billion.**
- NIKE directly manages its affiliate program.

Main **features** of your affiliate program:
- Up to **11% commission on** all valid sales.
- Cookies validity period: 30 days.
- Full range of category-specific affiliate banners.
- Nike By You specific promotional material.
- Frequent communications to affiliates regarding offers and new products.
- Gifts available for promotions and competitions in which affiliates participate.

Who can become a Nike affiliate? They are looking for sites of the following types:

- Sports sites
- Footwear/clothing/fashion sites
- News sites
- Fitness and health sites
- Sites with unique content
- Purchasing directories
- Blogs

What **advantages** can Nike affiliates offer customers?
- Free shipping on eligible orders.
- Periods of occasional offers.
- Customer promotions.
- Lower free shipping thresholds.

Information and registration to the NIKE affiliate program:
https://www.nike.com/us/es/help/a/programa-de-afiliados-de-nike

B.- Product developers

A person, company or organization creates a product and the affiliate program to spread the word and try to trigger sales.
Pays a commission to the affiliate for each transaction obtained through your affiliate link.

Example. iebschool.com

IEBS is a European training center that is committed to the future by training leading professionals capable of innovation and entrepreneurship, bringing value to their companies, their employees and society in general.

The iebschool.**com** training center offers an affiliate program. How does your affiliate program work?
- Once you sign up as a partner they send you creatives and product lists.
- You will be assigned a referral code that will be added to the IEBS URL. It is your identifier. Your affiliate link.
- You have access to an interface where you will be able to see at any time the leads obtained.
- Each month you will receive the amount corresponding to the leads obtained.

- It guarantees you income forever. That is, if a user registers and makes a subsequent purchase, you also receive remuneration for it.

Addressed to:
- Associations.
- Teachers.
- Blogs and websites

C.- Salesman.

It is a website that sells products to the end customer. In many cases it is a marketplace. This is a very common figure in affiliate marketing.

Example
1. Marketplace. Amazon Associates

Amazon Associates is Amazon's affiliate marketing program. It helps content creators, publishers and bloggers monetize their traffic.

With millions of products and programs available on Amazon, associates use simple link building tools to direct their audience to their recommendations and earn money on qualifying purchases and programs.

Steps to make money with Amazon Associates:

1.- Sign up. You become part of the tens of thousands of creators, publishers and bloggers who earn income with the Amazon Associates Program.

2.- You recommend. You are able to share millions of products with your audience of followers.

3.- You earn. You can earn up to **10%** commissions on qualifying purchases and programs.

Amazon Associates program registration: https://affiliate-program.amazon.com/

Example 2. Ecommerce. www.platanomelon.com
It is an online store of erotic products. It has a monthly traffic of 1 million visits (2021).

Main features of your affiliate program:
- 7% commission on each sale
- Duration of cookies: 30 days

Examples of **content** in your blog (eroteca):
- Menstrual panties: use and benefits
- Which hormonal contraceptive method best suits you? Are they for you?
- Advantages of doing it (intercourse) in socks

2.- Affiliate

*Imagine the **San Francisco Bay**. On one shore are the merchants with their products and on the other shore are the customers.*
*The affiliate is the **Golden Gate Bridge**, the **bridge** that connects the two shores.*
*Its structure and framework is made up of honest opinions, useful content, **affiliate links** and referral traffic to the merchant's website.*
*The affiliate is the company or person who **promotes** the merchant's products, will get the commission, which will be paid by the merchant when the sale takes place, will earn "**Golden Money**", continuing with the metaphor :)*

The affiliate is an intermediary, a commission agent who sends traffic to the merchant's website and gets a reward (profit) in the form of a commission.

To be successful in affiliate marketing, in addition to actions aimed at creating content and promoting products, you have to undertake a number of tasks. The most important are:
- Know yourself. Be clear about their interests, what attracts them, what they like, what excites them, what they know or what they want to learn.
- Knowing which niche to attack.

- Choose an affiliation program.
- Decide which products to promote.
- Choose the communication channel(s) on which you will focus your activity.
- Produce and publish content that is valuable, useful, relevant and unique.
- Generate traffic through the channel(s).
- Create community.
- Refer traffic to the merchant's website.
- Drive conversions.
- Monetize.
- Collect commissions.

Key idea

The affiliate's main task is to **promote** the merchant's products.

Your best weapon is **useful, relevant** and **unique content.**

The reward is to get traffic, refer them to the merchant's website and get commissions on sales.

"We need to stop interrupting people's content of interest and become their content of interest."

Craig Davis

"It's much easier to boost your business by doubling your conversion rate than by doubling your traffic."

Jeff Eisenberg

3.- Customer

It's the buyer, the payer. The fuel that provides the necessary energy for the whole affiliate marketing machine to work. If there are no sales, the customer does not pull the card, there are no conversions, no commissions for the affiliate. Total failure.

No matter how excellent the niche, no matter how high the traffic, if at the end of the whole process, the customer does not buy, the affiliate marketing business does not work.

No sales. No profit. No business.

Honesty. Always treat your customers **honestly**. Be honest with your users and potential customers, inform your community that your website includes affiliate links, and that you may receive a small commission if they buy the product you recommend.

Sincerity and honesty increase your credibility.

There are countries that include in their legal system the obligation to inform users about this aspect.

"Honesty is the first chapter in the book of wisdom."
                                        Thomas Jefferson

"Whoever does not take the truth seriously in small matters, cannot be trusted in big matters either."
                                        Albert Einstein

Example
*The disclaimer **and disclaimer** contained in*
www.younghouselove.com.

Remember this is about the successful decorating and DIY blog created by **John and Sherry**. It goes like this...

"Young House Love includes relevant affiliate links (both in content and in the sidebar), all of which we do our best to clearly mark as such.

As an Amazon associate, we earn on qualifying purchases (meaning that if you click on an affiliate link and make a purchase, we may receive a small commission).

This involves NO additional cost to you, and the affiliate money we earn helps pay the fees to keep this site up and running. Thank you for your support!

No giveaways or special blogger discounts are accepted, and none of the posts are sponsored."

www.younghouselove.com

"Whatever you do, do it so well that they come back and also bring their friends."

Walt Disney

4.- Affiliation networks

Affiliate networks are platforms that intermediate between affiliates and merchants.

They connect merchant websites (owning products), with content creators (affiliates promoting products).

Affiliate networks are a sort of Marketplace of affiliate programs, where you can find a great variety. They are sorted by category.

Best affiliate networks for marketers:
- ShareASale
- AWIN
- tradetracker.com
- CJ Affiliate
- ClickBank
- FlexOffers
- Avangate Affiliate Network
- Rakuten Advertising
- Impact
- affiliaXe
- GiddyUp
- Shopify Collabs

Examples of affiliate networks:
A- www.awin.com/es

Awin in figures:
- **920 million** euros paid to affiliates in the last financial year
- 15 offices worldwide
- 1,000 employees
- 225,000 members
- 16,500 traders

Source: https://www.awin.com/es/sobre-nosotros

Affiliate programs that you can find on awin.com:
- https://www.sephora.com/beauty/affiliates (cosmetics)
- happysocks.com/en (socks, masks, swimsuits...)

- etam.es (intimate apparel)
- interrail.eu/en (sale of vouchers to travel in europe by train)
- hawkersco.com/ (Hawkers. Sunglasses.)
- tennis-point.com (tennis and paddle products)
- tusloteras.es (online lottery administration)
- kappastore.es (sports and lifestyle clothing)
- pandora.net/en (jewelry)
- myspringfield.com/en (fashion)

Its advertiser directory lists affiliate programs in the following **categories:**

Finance and insurance
- Credit cards
- Insurance
- Loans
- Mortgages
- Personal Banking
- Savings and investments

Retail and Shopping
- Audiovisual
- Automotive
- Babies and children
- Books and subscriptions
- Children's clothing
- Clothing
- Clothing accessories
- Computers
- Department stores
- Do-it-yourself
- Electronic accessories
- Electronics store
- Entertainment store
- Erotic
- FMCG
- Furniture
- Electronic devices

- Gifts and flowers
- Ecological
- Group purchase
- Health and beauty
- Home and gardening
- Jewelry
- Lead generation
- Lingerie
- Men's clothing
- Music and DVD
- Office supplies
- Computers and video games
- Companion animals
- Medications
- Photography
- Photos and printing services
- Shoes
- Sports equipment
- Sportswear
- Toys and games
- Menaje
- Wine, alcohol and tobacco
- Women's clothing

Telecommunications and services
- B2B Utility Company
- B2B business services
- Cable and satellite operators
- Charity
- Quotations
- Digital TV and video on demand
- Education, training and recruitment
- Entertainment downloads
- Bets and competitions
- Internet Service Provider
- Lead generation
- Mobile broadband
- Mobile contract
- Mobile downloads

- Mobile payment in the period
- Network operators
- Online games
- Software downloads
- Tickets
- Public utilities company
- Web hosting
- itura

Travel
- Airlines
- Airport parking and transfers
- Vehicle rental
- Buses
- Cruises and ferries
- Hotels and lodging
- Lead generation
- Local festivals
- Tourism and attractions
- Trains
- Travel Agencies

Other interesting affiliate platforms that you should consider are:

B- tradetracker.com/en/campaigns/en

Platform with more than 250 advertisers - merchants. It has a wide variety of affiliate programs.

Categories with programs in Tradetracker:
- Adult
- Food and beverage
- Animals
- Art and life
- Babies and children
- Quotations
- Cars, motorcycles, motorcycles

- Sports and recreation
- Appliances
- Employment, education and career
- Flowers
- Hardware and software
- Hobbies and free time
- Home and garden
- Games and fun
- Toys
- Books, newspapers and magazines
- Lottery and betting
- Fashion and jewelry
- Music, video and DVD
- Domain names and hosting
- Office
- Other
- Financial products
- Gifts and gadgets
- Health and beauty
- Professional Services
- Telecommunications
- Stores
- Travel and vacations

More affiliate networks you should study, among all of them you will find the program or programs that fit your preferences and objectives. We highlight:
- https://account.admitad.com/es/catalog/
- https://www.shareasale.com/info/
- https://www.tradedoubler.com/es/
- https://www.timeone.io/es
- https://rakutenadvertising.com/
- https://www.cj.com/es/afiliado
- https://www.flexoffers.com/
- https://skimlinks.com/
- https://www.2checkout.com/
- https://www.linkconnector.com/
- https://warriorplus.com/

I do not review each one of them because we would make this book endless.

Depending on your interests and niche, research each of them and find affiliate programs that fit your goals. There are thousands. Do your research.

Example. Leroy Merlin

Let's take a look at an example of an affiliate program promoted by the **awin** affiliate network: the **Leroy Merlin** affiliate program.

Leroy Merlin is a French multinational company specializing in DIY, construction, decoration and gardening installed in **13 countries.**

Features of the **Leroy Merlin** affiliate program:
- Commission rate: **6%** and possibility of obtaining incentives based on performance and quality of collaboration.
- Extensive catalog. More than **180,000 products.**
- A multitude of options to generate quality content
- New materials for creators, authors and bloggers
- The program has a 30-day post-click attribution window (this is the duration of the cookies).

$ $ $ $ $

Part 2. Market niches

What is a niche market and how to choose one?

A niche market is a set of consumers with shared concerns, problems, interests and hobbies.

They are a part of the market, a portion. They are customers with common characteristics. The **three characteristics** that define a niche market are:

1.- It is a **portion of the market**, a segment, a piece, a part.
2.- It encompasses a **group** of consumers who share **common interests**.
3.- **Profitable**. It has enough critical mass. There is a **significant number of people interested in it,** a sufficient number of users to be able to monetize all our efforts in affiliate marketing.

Examples of niche markets:
- Adults only hotels
- Pet friendly hotels
- Prefabricated wooden houses
- Lovers of organic products
- Moms using reusable diapers
- Wooden toys for children from 2 to 5 years old
- Educational toys for girls from 3 to 7 years old
- Accessories for runners
- Articles for tennis players
- Everything you need for padel enthusiasts
- Automatic shirt ironers
- People concerned about the security of their properties
- Grand Theft Auto V players
- Nintendo Switch universe players
- Passionate about Playstation 5

The possibilities are endless. Search and create your path

The 5 key aspects to consider when choosing a niche market

First. Well defined. The market niche must be concrete, specific, they have a common problem, a specific need, or they are united by an interest, example of niches:
- Dwarf rabbit lovers
- Indian motorcycle owners
- Running practitioners
- NBA lovers
- Republican voters (USA)
- Democratic voters (USA)
- Owners of Beagle breed dogs...

Second. Pioneering. Look for untapped niches. Explore new spaces and galaxies, there is a whole universe out there to discover. Don't be one more with typical products oriented to users of:
- Apple
- Samsung
- Xiaomi..., and similar

These are well-worn niches, with high competition, difficult to stand out and position. Be creative.

Third. Perennial. Segment that generates interest in a permanent and sustained manner over time. Do not invest time in a niche that responds to a passing fad.

Google provides us with an excellent tool that allows us to analyze whether a niche is a stable trend over time or not. https://trends.google.es/trends

Example of niche: DOG TOYS, the Google Trends graph indicates that:
1.- There is an **increase in** the trend over the last 5 years.
2.- There are **peaks** in searches during the **Christmas campaigns** of the last 5 years.

Fourth. Create community. I insist.
Your efforts as an affiliate should be focused on creating and leading a community.

More examples of niche markets, of communities that you can create, help, advise and lead.
- Lovers of the Labrador dog breed
- Owners of the German Shepherd breed
- Dog lovers in general
- Passionate about parakeets
- Motorcycle lovers
- Campers
- Hikers
- Pilgrims on the Camino de Santiago
- Consumers concerned about savings
- Consumers seeking to maximize their financial investments
- Star Wars saga lovers
- Star Trek fans
- Galactica Passionate. Battlestar
- Chess scholars
- Basketball players... ... ...

Fifth. Profitable. It is when there is sufficient profit potential to make our efforts profitable and we can achieve the financial objectives we have set for ourselves.

$ $ $ $ $

Market niche. Demand and competitiveness

1.- Demand

The niche market has to be specific, but we also need to have **enough demand**. That is, with enough potential buyers to make our affiliate marketing efforts profitable.

Critical mass exists when there is a minimum number of potential buyers and we can achieve our financial objectives.

How do you know if there is enough demand?
An excellent **starting point to** find out whether or not there is demand is to research the **monthly search volume** for the keywords that serve to identify our market niche.

Which tool is useful? Use the Google keyword planner to find out the monthly search volume of the keyword (keywords):

https://ads.google.com/intl/es_es/home/tools/keyword-planner

The following link takes you to a page with a comprehensive and simple explanation to help you get the most out of this excellent tool

https://support.google.com/google-ads/answer/Cómo use keyword planner

Based on the number of monthly visits for the keywords important to your niche market you can estimate the profit potential of your niche blog.

Keyword Surfer

Another excellent tool is **Keyword Surfer**, it is a browser extension (chrome), easy to use and when you search in Google it provides information on search volume, keyword ideas and similarity percentage.

Keyword Surfer is free. Free. You can find and install it at:
https://chrome.google.com/webstore/search/keyword%20surfer

Competitiveness.
Competitiveness is the difficulty that each keyword has to position itself in the first places in Google's results page.

The **Google AdWords** keyword planner classifies keywords between low and high competitiveness.
- **Competitiveness is low.** It is easy to appear in the first positions in Google.
- **High competitiveness.** It is not easy to rank content at the top, we will have to compete with digital empires like Amazon and the like.

Example of search and keyword volume analysis. Profitability analysis

Case study

The story of Mister Ship (Fish breeding enthusiast). **Mr. Ship** is an aquarium hobbyist. He loves everything related to the breeding and care of fish in an aquarium.

You want to start an affiliate marketing business. He has thought it would be an excellent option to launch a blog with tips for aquarium fish keeping hobbyists.

Mr. Ship researches the **keyword volume** in Google keyword planner and keyword Surfer, between the two tools he obtains the following results and data (USA):

NO.	Key words	Monthly search volume
1	**aquariums**	**50.000**
2	fish tanks	50.000
3	**water turtle**	**9.100**
4	water turtle	8.100
5	fish tank	6.600
6	**aquarium fish**	**2.900**
7	aquarium with fish	2.900
8	fish and aquariums	2.900

9	marine aquarium	2.900
10	**small fish tanks**	**2.400**
11	large tortoise	1.900
12	cheap fish tank	1.900
13	cheap fish tanks	1.900
14	large turtles	1.900
15	aquarium decoration	1.900
16	large fish tanks	1.600
17	amazon fish tanks	1.300
18	cheap aquarium	1.300
19	aquariums buy	1.300
20	buy aquarium	1.300
21	fish tank with fish	1.300
22	small turtle	1.300
23	small turtles	1.300
24	turtle tanks	1.000
25	aquariums for turtles	1.000
26	fish tanks	880
27	round fish tanks	880
28	large aquarium	880
29	large aquariums	880
30	fish tank	880
31	fish tank	880
32	fish tank decoration	880
33	fish tanks and aquariums	590
34	fish tanks prices	210
35	round glass fish	210

	tanks	
36	houses with fish tanks	170
37	homemade fish tanks	140
38	giant fish tanks	140
39	large round fish tank	140
40	cheap large fish tanks	140
41	small round fish tank	110
42	buy large aquarium	70
43	pictures of fish tanks	70
	Total searches	**201.650**

Source: Keyword Surfer

Mister Ship, after this study, knows the search volumes of the various keywords related to the aquarium world.

Once **Mr Ship** knows the **search volume of the** keywords, the next step is to study the level of competition it has.

The level of competition (remember) indicates the difficulty of being able to position these terms in the first search results in Google.

Competitiveness:
Google's keyword planner indicates the level of competitiveness of each keyword or set of keywords.

Classified in:
High competition. It is difficult to position the term in the first Google search results, we will have to fight against giants such as Amazon, "Mission Almost Impossible".

Low competition. Indicates the opposite. It is easy to rank high in Google. We will focus our efforts on these terms.

Medium competition. It will not be easy to position our keywords, but with a good job we will obtain positive results.

Mr. Ship does the study and obtains the following information. Table information obtained from:
- Keyword Surfer
- Google Ads Keyword Planner)
- Data for Spain only

Keywords	Monthly volume	Competition
aquariums	50.000	Download
fish store near me	500	Download
monterrey aquarium	500	Download
aquariums in mexico	500	Download
aquarium near me	5.000	Download
aquarium near me	50	Download
aquarium park	50	Download
aquarium store	50	Download
tropical fish stores	50	Download
fish tanks	50.000	High
aquarium accessories	50	High
fish tanks at walmart	500	High
lobelia cardinalis aquarium	500	High
sale of fish online usa	50	High
petsmart fish tanks	500	High

turtle tanks at walmart	50	High
small fish tanks walmart	50	High
biobola	50	High
10 gallon fish tank filter	50	High
20 gallon fish tank filter	50	High
30 gallon fish tanks	50	High
fish tank filters at walmart	50	High
fish tanks at petsmart	500	High
fish tank ornaments at walmart	50	High
20 gallon walmart fish tank	50	High
55 gallon fish tank filter	50	High
walmart large fish tanks	50	High
walmart 10 gallon fish tank	50	High
75 gallon fish tank	50	High
40 gallon fish tanks	50	High
walmart fish tank filters	50	High
150 gallon fish tank	50	High
55 gallon fish tanks	50	High

Mister Ship has discovered a term with sufficient search volume and a low level of competition and will focus its efforts on it.

The winner is:

Keyword	Volume / monthly	Competition
aquariums	50.000	Download

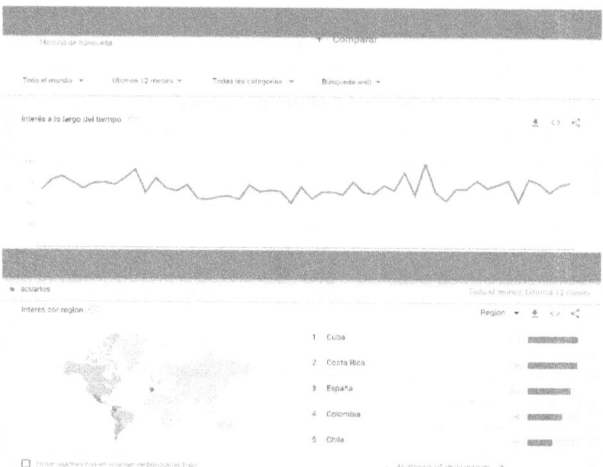

The keyword **"AQUARIUMS"** has sufficient search volume, is in demand (sufficient **critical mass: 50,000** monthly searches in Spain alone) and has **low competition**. It is feasible to position our content in the top positions of Google for this keyword:

Let's analyze the overall trend, over time, for this search term "aquarium". Remember that we use **Google Trends** to find out this information.

Highlights:
- The number of searches remains stable throughout the year with spikes in August and early March.
- The searches in **Spain,** Cuba, Costa Rica, Colombia, Chile and Mexico are significant.
- In the Google Ads keyword planner we can find out the number of searches in each of its countries. This information will be useful if we want to make a small advertising

investment in Facebook Ads to accelerate our affiliate marketing results.

Summary:
Volume: 50,000 monthly searches in the Spanish market alone.
Competence. Low level. Easy to position in the first five positions in Google.

Volume + Low competition
=
High probability of success

Estimation of benefits.
- **Mister Ship** believes that with its unique value content it can capture **30%** to **50%** of organic traffic.
- Expected conversion rate: 3%.
- You will obtain between 150 and 250 sales each month
- Commission: 5 € per sale (average)
- Estimated profit: **Between 2,250 € and 3,750 €.**

The hobby of keeping fish in a Mister Ship aquarium is going from being a hobby to a business model.
Thanks to affiliate marketing

Act

- Create your list of niches and related keywords
  Do you enjoy camping? How about creating a blog providing excellent advice to campers? Does it make sense to you? Of course it makes sense.
- **The Google AdWords** keyword planner analyzes the search volume and competitiveness of each keyword.
- Also use Keyword Surfer to obtain accurate search volumes by country and new suggested words.
- Export the data to a spreadsheet to make hypotheses following the Mister Ship methodology.

$ $ $ $ $

250 market niches

Let's look at several examples of niche markets. This is a list only as an example. There are as many options as you want. It is a universe with infinite possibilities. Take advantage of them.
Niches by **product category:**

Garden
- Outdoor storage
- Birds and garden animals
- Barbecue and outdoor dining
- Heaters, campfires and fireplaces
- Lawn mowers and outdoor power tools
- Covers and fences
- Outdoor decoration
- Gardening
- Garden furniture and accessories
- Swimming pools, hot tubs and supplies
- Plants, seeds and bulbs
- Thermometers and meteorological instruments

Supplements for athletes: medications, remedies and dietary supplements
Health and personal care
- Baby and childcare
- Welfare
- Oral care
- Health care
- Eye care
- Home care and cleaning
- Diet and nutrition
- Smoking devices and accessories
- Intimate hygiene
- Sex and sensuality
- Medical supplies and equipment
- Vitamins, minerals and supplements

Watches.
- Man
- Wristwatches
- Smartwatches Fashion
- Pocket watches
- Belts
- Sports watches
- Interesting watches
- Analog watches
- Digital watches
- Antique clocks
- Star Wars Watches

Baby
- Diapers
- Ecological diapers
- Strollers and baby carriages
- Pacifiers and teethers
- Rest and sleep
- Hygiene and care
- Breastfeeding and feeding
- Urinals and stools
- Walk
- Gifts for newborns
- Maternity clothes
- Security
- Car seats and accessories
- Baby shoes
- Baby toys

Nutritional drinks for athletes
- Protein drinks
- Recovery and hydration drinks
- Energy drinks
- Drinks for weight control

Vegan world
- Candies
- Protein shakes
- Chocolates
- Cereals
- Books, ebooks on vegan topics
- Sweets
- Vitamin supplements
- Butter

Beauty
- Shaving and depilation
- Bathroom and personal hygiene
- Skin care
- Hair care
- Manicure and pedicure
- Makeup
- Perfumes and fragrances
- Utensils and accessories

Swimming pools
- Prefabricated pools
- Small pools
- Demountable pools
- Inflatable pools
- Integrated pools
- Swimming pools

Swimming pool supplies
- Heaters and accessories
- Garden showers
- Filters, pumps and accessories
- Covers and accessories
- Cleaning tools and accessories
- Jacuzzis and SPAs
- Repair kits
- Paints and sealing products
- Swimming pools

- Cleaning products
- Safety products
- Lighting products
- Chemical and water analysis products
- Outdoor saunas and parts
- Thermometers
- Slides, ladders and trampolines

Sports Universe
- Running
- Cycling
- Swimming
- Diving
- River fishing
- Sea fishing
- Hunting
- Airsoft
- Survival
- Trekking
- Camping
- Basketball
- Soccer
- Indoor soccer
- Badminton
- Paddle
- Tennis
- Table tennis
- Cycling
- Sportswear
- Technology for sports
- Food and supplements for athletes
- Yoga
- Fitness
- Bodybuilding

2.- Classification based on interests:
- Recycling
- Healthy living
- Organic products
- Vegan cuisine
- Detox
- Passionate about travel
- Bicycle routes
- Caravan routes
- Camper and van tours
- Solo travel
- Nature lovers
- New parents
- Animal cruelty-free makeup products

Hobbies and interests:
- DYI. Do it yourself
- Crafts
- Children's handicrafts
- Wood crafts
- Painting with watercolor
- Oil painting
- Painting landscapes
- Painting portraits
- Art on paper
- Video games
- Retro video games
- Nintendo Switch video games
- PS4 Video Games
- Strategy video games
- Video game xbox one
- Video games develop skills
- Strategy video games
- Board games
- Retro board games
- Monument models
- Fighter aircraft models
- Model of passenger transport aircraft

- Tank models
- Model ships
- Wooden ship models
- Aeromodelismo
- Drones
- Puzzles
- Motoring enthusiasts
- Motorcycling fans
- Cycling enthusiasts
- Military fashion

Within the niche of **motoring** enthusiasts:
- Car accessories
- Car and motorcycle care. Oils and other fluids
- GPS devices
- Vehicle electronics
- Car tools
- Tires and wheels
- Car parts
- Paint and painting accessories
- Products for hobbyists
- Car seats and accessories
- Transportation and storage

3.- Classification of niches in alphabetical order.
- Audio accessories
- Bathroom fixtures and accessories
- Wedding accessories
- Camping and hiking accessories
- Hunting accessories
- Cycling accessories
- Car accessories
- Photography and camera accessories
- Lighting fixtures and accessories
- Motorcycle accessories
- Video accessories
- Video game accessories
- Accessories for action cameras
- Hair accessories

- Men's accessories
- Telephone accessories
- Home storage and organization
- Anime
- Wall art and decoration
- Men's restroom
- Headphones and Earphones
- Energy banks
- Solar energy banks
- Bath and body
- Bar
- Binoculars and Optics
- Cosmetic Bags and Organizers
- Camping bags and backpacks
- Evening and party bags
- Travel bags and backpacks
- Sports bags and backpacks
- Women's handbags and purses
- Men's handbags and wallets
- Bustiers and Corsets
- Audio and video cables and adapters
- TV Boxes
- Telephone boxes
- Women's hosiery
- Socks
- Printed T-shirts
- Solar chargers
- Posters
- Textile house
- Cocktail and party dresses
- Electronic components
- Cosplay
- Cutlery and Flatware
- Magic Cubes and Puzzles
- Skin care and treatments
- Health care
- Hair care and treatments
- Dental care

- Sewing
- Home Decoration
- Drawing
- Data storage devices
- Health monitoring devices
- Drones
- Office electronics
- Household Electronics and Appliances
- Pregnancy and maternity products
- Winter sports equipment and accessories
- Laboratory equipment
- Swimming equipment
- Safety equipment
- Sports equipment
- Eyelash extensions
- Girdles
- Fan Merch
- Water filters
- Artificial flowers
- Mobile photography
- Wireless Gadgets
- Sunglasses
- GoPro
- Kitchen faucets
- Kitchen tools
- Styling tools
- Automotive repair tools
- Power Tools and Accessories
- Hand tools and accessories
- Feminine hygiene
- Baking
- 3D Printers
- Measuring instruments
- Women's jewelry
- Jewelry for men
- Wedding jewelry
- Fine jewelry
- Toys
- Baby toys

- Construction toys
- Remote control toys
- Educational toys
- Batteries
- Flashlights
- Chain lights
- Permanent make-up
- Massagers
- Home improvement
- Microscopes
- Watch straps and bands
- Backpacks
- USB charging backpacks
- Baby monitors
- Intimate women
- Dolls and dollhouses
- Narghile
- Pocket knives
- Stationery
- Parts of a computer
- Wigs and Hair Extensions
- Computer peripherals
- Fishing
- genuine leather
- Orthopedic insoles
- Gaiters
- Jewelry production
- Shaving and hair removal products
- Makeup products
- Baby care products
- Sexual products
- Projectors and projector accessories
- Charms Bracelet
- GPS Trackers
- Smart watches and bracelets
- Watches
- Wooden clocks
- Music players

- Robots
- Dancewear and shoes
- Men's clothing
- Women's clothing
- Sportswear
- 3D printed clothing
- Men's underwear
- Military clothing and accessories
- Baby and children's clothing
- Baby safety
- Smart home security systems
- Hats and caps
- Sony PlayStation
- Nail art supplies
- Arts and Crafts Supplies
- Household cleaning supplies
- Pet supplies
- Party supplies
- Drawing tablets
- Large sizes
- Temporary tattoos
- Cell phones
- Bathroom textiles
- Bedroom textiles and bedding
- Tie Dye
- Utensils
- Vape and electronic cigarettes
- Wedding dresses
- Yoga
- Sneakers
- Baby and children's shoes
- Men's shoes

As you have seen, the options are many, varied and infinite. Search and decide which niches you like, are of your interest.

Key idea
Behind every community with common interests, if there is enough critical mass of users (demand), you are sure to find merchants with affiliate programs that offer products that meet this unsatisfied demand.

In these examples we have explored a tiny part of the categories, niches and micro-niches that can be the focus of your affiliate marketing strategy.

Find your own niche with imagination. Be creative. Show the world that you are different, that your approach is different. Be good. Be unique. Create your uniqueness.

Remember...
If you are just one more. You will be irrelevant
Be different. Be unique. Be daring.

Challenge
- Detect a niche, a community with common interests. Remember that ideally, this interest should coincide with a hobby of yours. You should also be interested in it.
- Study if there is demand. Sufficient critical mass (volume). Use Google Ads keyword planner and Keyword Surfer (both free).
- Analyzes the level of competitiveness. Low, High or Medium

Finally, dear marketer, if you want to amuse yourself by counting the number of niches listed in this chapter, you will see that there are well over 250, but we were not going to let a cold and dreary figure prevent us from giving this chapter a nice, rounded title:

The 250...
Well, OK. OK. The 250 + VAT :)

Time to act

1. Elaborate a list of interests (niches). Minimum 5
2. Do a keyword research study
    a. Number
    b. Competitiveness
    c. Make several earnings assumptions in an excel sheet
3. Look for solvent merchants with affiliate programs. Analyze the basic features: commissions, cookie duration (...)

$ $ $ $ $

Part 3. Criteria for choosing affiliate programs

How to Choose the Right Affiliate Program: 7 Keys to Success

Choosing the affiliate program we are going to work with is an **important** decision, the selected one will be your partner. The duration of the relationship is long term, he will pay your commissions and in his hands lies, to a large extent, your financial security and stability.

You create valuable content, generate community, send traffic and the merchant who owns the affiliate program sets the program and conditions, product, sales, logistics, customer service and pays your commissions.

Let's proceed to analyze the different aspects that you should consider when choosing an affiliate program and products to promote.

The 7 keys are:

Key 1. Reputation of the affiliate program owner
Betting on an affiliate program is a partnership. It is preferable that this relationship is with:
- Well-established traders
- Operate in the market for a long time
- Holders of a reputable affiliate program with good reputation
- Have high monthly traffic to your website. Ranked among the leaders in your sector
- Consolidated sales
- Provide financial soundness. That we do not have problems to collect our commissions.
- Reputable. Excellent reviews and feedback from affiliates who have been working with this provider for a long time.

Key 2. Love. Enjoy

Fall in love. Select products you love. Your affiliate marketing business is going to take time and effort. Make it easy, choose programs and products that you enjoy, for example:
- Do you enjoy your pet, your Labrador, how about the zooplus or petplan.es (pet insurance) affiliate program, or both, since they are complementary?
- Are you an athlete? Shall we try the Decathlon or Kappa affiliate program?

You see the point, don't you?

Key 3. Adored by your target audience

Your users have a number of common characteristics, such as demographics, interests, hobbies, passions...

The content you share and the information you disseminate on your blog or website must be of quality, relevant and interesting for your community. In this sense, the products you recommend must also be attractive and desired by your target audience.

Recommend products that arouse their curiosity, their desire to buy them, because otherwise there will be no traffic to your affiliate links, nor to the merchant's website, nor will you have conversions, nor commissions. Nothing.

Key 4. Show me the dough. Yield. Profitability

The ultimate goal of all your affiliate marketing efforts is to monetize. Seek to earn a return.

You want the effort, performance and results of all the actions you are carrying out to bring you sufficient income. Receive commissions. Meet your income objectives.

The affiliate program you work with must have the potential for economic return, which is able to justify all the effort and dedication you put into it.

Make calculations, create hypotheses based on expected traffic, average conversion rate, profit per sale and with all these assumptions find out the potential revenue you can get if all these conditions are met.

Depending on the type of blog and content provided, you will have to choose the affiliate program or programs with which you are going to collaborate. I insist. Make numbers. Make hypotheses, consider different scenarios. Hypotheses that may occur:
- **Few sales** and high profit in each one of them
- **Many sales** with lower individual profit
- **High sales** and high commission rate

Key 5. Recurring commissions. Show me the money on a regular basis.

Is there anything better than converting traffic into a sale and earning a commission? Yes, getting **recurring revenue,** month after month.

Recurring revenue allows the effort of acquiring a customer to periodically report income in your current account.

Isn't it wonderful? It's the nirvana of passive income. You work once and get paid every month. You earn income periodically, for as long as the business relationship lasts.

Example of a program with recurring income
Datacenter1

Features of the Datacenter affiliate program1:
- 100% Managed Hosting.
- Commission of 16.66%.
- Lifetime commission. Recurring income
- Cookie duration: 90 days
    Information: https://cdn.datacenter1.com

Key 6. Product quality and Honesty

If the product we promote is not of quality, we will lose credibility and influence over our community.

Every time we recommend a product, we put our reputation at stake. Given the vast number of programs and products at our disposal, it makes no sense to bet on items of dubious quality or that may generate problems in the future. Don't do it. Go for programs and products that will generate satisfied customers.

Happy customers = Loyal users

Remember that your **reputation, your brand, your source of income** is at stake.

Anecdote

I am reminded of a post I read advising the **3 best microphones** to record podcasts. The blogger in his article analyzes several microphones and monetizes the content of his website with Amazon's affiliate program (Amazon Associates).

What was my surprise when among the hundreds of microphones that were available on Amazon to promote, **I recommended three poorly rated in this marketplace,** with scores below 4.

What credibility does a blogger have with this kind of advice and reviews? How is it possible that having dozens of microphones with good ratings, he advises three poorly rated microphones? Desidia? Bad faith perhaps? Maybe he advised expensive microphones to raise the amount of his commission? Is it a lack of **honesty**?

This blogger is either a bad professional, a bad person or both. Bad, very bad.

*DON'T DO IT. BE HONEST. BE PROFESSIONAL.
EVERYTHING YOU DO AND DON'T DO BUILDS YOUR BRAND.
DEFINE YOU*

Key 7. Excellent customer service

In addition to checking that the products are of proven quality, we must also check for excellence in the customer service provided by the merchant.

What happens if a problem arises, does the vendor neglect or does it have a reputation for excellent customer service? Every dissatisfied customer undermines our credibility.

Read the reviews that the supplier has, what opinions do users have about their products and about the customer service they provide. Is it well rated? Does it deal quickly and promptly with any incidents?

Analyze the rating and score of the merchant on social networks, on google, read reviews and comments.

> "Affiliate marketing is not just about promoting products, it's about building relationships with your audience and providing value to them."

$ $ $ $

The right price

How much should the products we promote be?

In the TV quiz show: "THE RIGHT PRICE", contestants compete to guess the price of a product. The winner is the one who comes closest. Without overdoing it.

Let's see, without going too far or too short, within what price range the products we promote should fluctuate. What price should the products we promote and those we expect to commission have?

General principle
The more expensive the products and the higher the commission, the more money we earn.

Mr. and Mrs. Obviousness :)

In addition to the "brainy" contribution of Mr. and Mrs. Obvious (thank you), there are **three reflections** you should make when choosing which products to promote based on the **price** and the commission you can obtain:

1.- Impulse buying vs. reflexive buying.

Affiliation programs are associated with tracking through cookies, which have a duration of validity ranging from 24 hours (Amazon Associates) to 7, 30, 60, 120 days or more.

Cookies, tracking, how? Let me explain, every time an Internet user follows one of your affiliate links to the merchant's website, a "tracker" is installed on their device, this is the cookie, which sends information to the merchant.

Each affiliation program gives its cookies a **period of duration**, of **expiration** and, once it is lost, the right to charge the commission expires even if the sale takes place.

As the price of the product increases, the more time the customer needs to make a purchase decision. They will want to gather information, make comparisons on different websites, meditate, consult...

Buying a phone case has nothing to do with buying a phone. The case is an impulse purchase, while the purchase of a smartphone is reflexive and takes time. Longer periods of time go against the lifespan of your cookie.

Example

Computer with Pvp: 1.500 €. Commission 4%: Amount obtained: 60 € vs.

External memory of 2 terabytes. Pvp: 69 €. Commission 4% Amount obtained: 2.76 euros.

A priori it seems a better option to promote computers, but be careful. Be careful. As it is a reflexive purchase, which has to mature, it can be that our cookie expires, that is to say, the sale takes place but without commission for us. Bad business.

On the other hand, smaller products are usually impulse purchases, less reflexive, more sales are produced, faster and our cookie does not expire. We collect our commission. Good "Business".

In summary, you should take into account the time it takes, on average, to make a purchase decision and compare with the duration of the cookie.

Purchase decision time longer than the cookie duration = Bad business

"Promoting high-priced products can result in higher commissions, but it also requires a more robust strategy to earn customer trust."

Conversion rate.

This is the ratio obtained by dividing the number of users who buy by the number of users who are referred.

From your blog mejoresfundasiPhone.com you have sent to Amazon 3,500 users, of these 323 have bought a case for their iPhone.

The **"Conversion Rate"** in this example is:

(323 / 3.500) * 100 = 9,2%

9.2% of users referred to Amazon have purchased a holster, this is the **conversion rate**.

3.- Advisable price range

The price range of the products to be promoted by affiliate marketing should be between the following ranges:

30 € - 300 €

Above **300 €** the conversion rate will drop (reflexive buying) and below **30 €** your efforts will probably not be properly rewarded (low commission).

Key ideas

In order to choose a niche market, analyze the following variables and create several hypotheses in a spreadsheet:
- Estimated traffic
- Expected conversion rate
- Forecast revenues (commissions)
- Average purchase decision time. Impulse or reflexive
- Cookie lifetime
- Product prices and expected commission

With all this information, decide which products you are going to promote.

$ $ $ $ $

Part 4. Web and Traffic

How to create a good, beautiful and cheap affiliate website

The blog is the meeting point with your audience, it is your digital real estate investment, your online real estate, and you should treat it as such. As an affiliate **marketer**, the blog is the website where you are going to publish valuable content, tips, opinions, comparisons, listings. Quality, useful and unique information that helps our community.

Key idea

In the blog you don't write content. You provide solutions. You solve problems.

1 POST = 1 SOLUTION

Your blog seeks to add value, solve problems, generate a change, a transformation in people's lives, thanks to the unique and useful content that you publish and contribute to the community.

What you need to have your blog. Make it easy, fast and cheap

To launch the blog in which to host the valuable content you will create and share with our community, you need:

1.- Domain.
What is a domain? The domain is a fundamental part of your blog. It is your identity. It is your personal brand or company brand.

The domain name creates a first impression. Think carefully about which name to choose. Brainstorm, select, discard, analyze, search until you fall in love with one of the options.

Tips to keep in mind when choosing a domain name:
A.- Short.
- The domain the less characters it has the better, the easier it is for your audience to remember it.
- Easy to **remember** and pronounce

- Never use **registered trademarks** in your domain name.

You've created a blog to promote and commission with the sale of **Harley Davidson** items and in a show of imagination you think:
- It will be called...
www.all-harleydavidson.com
... and to sell like a motorcycle...

Don't do it. You'll get into legal trouble, for sure.

B.- Avoid hyphenated domains:
- vehiculos-ocasion.com
- vehicles_passion.com

C.- Do not include numbers:
- 1000announcements.com
- cars123.com

How much does the domain cost? At namecheap.com, at the moment of writing this book, registering a .com domain costs:
- 7.46 euros for the first year
- 10,90 € the renewal
- There is the option of contracting several years, in which case the initial discount of the first year is maintained, as shown in the image.

2.- Hosting
What is hosting? It is the place where your blog will be hosted. In namecheap.com at the time of this writing this book has excellent domain prices.

CMS. Options.
A CMS is a management system that allows you to create and manage the content of your blog (Content Management System).

There are several CMS options to build our blog. The most used are:
- **WordPress.org**
- Blogger.com

- Tumblr

Most bloggers use **WordPress.org**, this CMS allows full control over the design and appearance of the blog.

WordPress has a whole ecosystem of extensions that makes it possible to extend the functionality far beyond just having a blog. Virtually any need you have such as creating a store, a reservation center, a marketplace, a membership..., you can do it in Wordpress. The options are endless.

Most of the services and tools you need to use for your affiliate marketing business such as: email manager, landing pages, billing system..., are compatible with WordPress.

WordPress.org is free, you can download it without paying anything. The vast majority of hosting, web hosting, have a control panel that allows the installation of WordPress quickly and easily.

Make it easy, simple, fast and cheap
Do it in WordPress
Don't complicate your life.

4.- Template. Subject

The template is the design that sets the look and structure of your Wordpress blog. There are free and paid templates, so don't spend money on a paid theme to begin with.

You will find hundreds of excellent **free templates** following this link: https://es.wordpress.org/themes

Three excellent **free** themes **that I recommend** are:
1. https://es.wordpress.org/themes/oceanwp/
2. https://es.wordpress.org/themes/astra/
3. https://es.wordpress.org/themes/storefront/
   (You can download them by following the links):

5.- Design. Construction. Management

Designing, building and managing a WordPress website is easy. On Udemy and Youtube you have free tutorials (video courses), with everything you need to know to start your blog. Here are the links:
- https://www.udemy.com/wordpress_básico
- https://www.youtube.com/wordpress+basic

Visualize them and you will have your blog up and running in a few minutes.

6.- Extensions. Plugins. What they are. Which ones to install. Best free options. We are still Free :)

> A WordPress **plugin** is a program that extends and improves the basic functions of WordPress, our content manager.

Let's look at several plugins that you should install on your WordPress. All of them are free:

Security

Install iThemes Security to protect your WordPress from hackers, malware and ransomware attacks.

iThemes Security. **It provides** 30 ways to secure and protect your WordPress based blog.

On average, **30,000 new websites** are hacked every day. WordPress sites can be an easy target for attacks due to vulnerabilities in plugins, weak passwords and outdated software.
Most WordPress administrators don't know they are vulnerable. iThemes Security works to lock down WordPress, fix common holes, stop automated attacks, and strengthen user credentials.

There is a premium, paid version, but the free version is enough to get started.

You can download the plugin at the following link:
https://wordpress.org/plugins/better-wp-security/

SEO # Search Engine Optimization. Search Engine Optimization.

The **Yoast SEO** plugin **helps** millions of websites around the world **rank** higher in search engines. **Yoast SEO Free** contains everything you need to manage your SEO strategy.

Main features that we can highlight of this acclaimed plugin:
- It provides the best automatic SEO techniques, such as canonical URLs and meta tags.
- Create advanced XML sitemaps; they make it easier for Google to understand the structure of your site and make it easier to position the page in Google's top results.
- Deep integration with Schema.org enables search engines to understand web content.
- Faster load times for the entire website, due to an innovative way of managing data in WordPress.

Free plugin download:
https://es.wordpress.org/plugins/wordpress-seo/

Analytical

Making decisions in Affiliate Marketing without analyzing the numbers, the figures, the data of our business is like driving a Ferrari at 250 km/hour with blindfolded...

We need to examine the blog numbers, the key data of our affiliate marketing business relating to:
- Traffic information
- No. of visits
- Origin, demographics
- Page views
- Most visited pages
- Time spent on our website
- Most successful products
- Conversion Rate...

All of this is done in order to make the right decisions regarding the management of our affiliate website.

Google Analytics is the best tool to analyze our website traffic and make decisions. It is free and provides excellent information. Let's suppose that **Google Analytics** tells us that 70% of our visitors are women between 26 and 40 years old. With this information we can decide:
- Prioritize content creation for this market segment
- Expand product assortment and recommendations for that gender and age segment.
- When advertising on Facebook, to accelerate our affiliate marketing business, we will segment by gender and age taking into account these data.

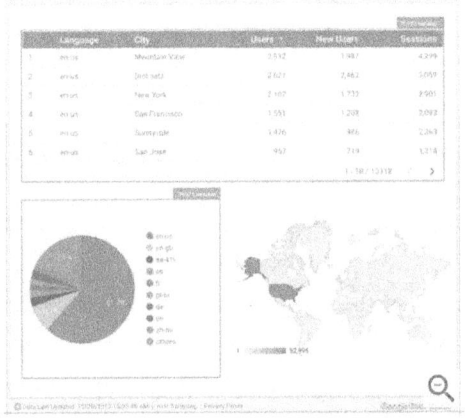

https://support.google.com

Recommended plugin to install the **Google Analytics code** in our blog is: **Better Google Analytics**

The **Better Google Analytics** add-on allows you to easily add Google Analytics code to your website and track all relevant information.

To download the free plugin: Better Google Analytics follow this link:
https://es.wordpress.org/plugins/better-analytics/

Tools to improve loading speed
The factors that influence the time it takes to load a website are:
- Quality hosting loads the blog faster.
- Lightweight templates and plugins.

- The page cache.
- Have optimized CSS, HTML and Javascript code.
- Lightweight images.

The loading speed of the website is a fundamental factor that affects the user experience. A page that takes too long to load increases the abandonment rate. The Internet user leaves. They don't have the patience to wait.

The loading speed also affects **SEO positioning.** Google's algorithm takes into account the loading time to position, better or worse, our content on the search engine results page.

It would be absurd to make a great effort in creating valuable, useful and unique content and have Google relegate it to the third or fourth page because our hosting is not of high quality and the blog takes a long time to load, or because of any other of the previous factors that we have seen and that influence the loading time.

How to reduce loading times. Follow these four simple steps:

First. Use Pingdom Tools (free) to find out how long it takes to load your website now, without optimizing.

An optimized website should take less than a second to load. This has to be your goal.

Second. Install extensions that improve cache performance. They are recommended:

- → **W3 Total Cache. W3 Total Cache** is a caching plugin for WordPress that helps to reduce web load time.
  W3 Total Cache reduces loading time thanks to:
  - Advanced cache configuration
  - Static file compression
  - Delayed load (lazy load)

  Free download of W3 Total Cache at:
  https://es.wordpress.org/plugins/w3-total-cache/

- → **WP Fastest Cache.** Alternative to W3 Total Cache. You can download it for free at:
  https://es.wordpress.org/plugins/wp-fastest-cache/

Third. Install a plugin to **optimize the images** on your website, so that they weigh less and load faster. Free plugins you can use:
- **EWWWW Image Optimizer:**
  https://es.wordpress.org/plugins/ewww-image-optimizer/
- Imsanity https://es.wordpress.org/plugins/imsanity/
- Smush https://es.wordpress.org/plugins/wp-smushit/

Follow these three steps and your website will load in less than a second. Impatient web surfers will not leave and Google will rank your content better.

Fourth. Hire a quality **hosting**. Analyze the expected loading time, if it is not good do not hire it or migrate your website to another one.

Don't let the loading time of your web site "load" your business. Keep this in mind

Create forms

For one reason or another you will need to create and publish forms on your website, for example for **contacting them.**

Recommended free extension: Contact Form 7

It is the most used and downloaded contact form plugin from the WordPress.org repository. It is free, easy to install and use. It allows:
- Manage multiple contact forms.
- Customize forms and mail content in a flexible way.
- The form supports Ajax technology submissions, CAPTCHA, Akismet spam filtering, etc.
- Create registration forms.
- Request for quotation
- Call me' buttons

Free download:
https://es.wordpress.org/plugins/contact-form-7/

Insert buttons to share in social networks

Using plugins that allow you to insert buttons to share content on social networks is an easy, fast and cheap way to make valuable content go viral, because it is easy to share with your audience and get free traffic to your website.

Allow your audience to distribute your content to social networks and instant messaging contacts at the click of a button.

Free and easy to use tool that allows you to create buttons to share content on social networks: **Sassy social Share**. It is a simple to configure extension. It includes buttons for all the social networks that exist. **Features:**
- Choose the size of the button you prefer.
- Choose colors for both the background and the border of the buttons.
- Choose the position where to place the buttons: sidebar, bottom, top, left, right...
- Decide on which pages you want the buttons to be displayed.
- Customize the shape of the buttons.
    - Circle
    - Square
    - Rectangle
- Responsive. Adapted to mobile devices.
- To be able to write the text you want.

Free download of **Sassy social Share** from:
https://wordpress.org/plugins/sassy-social-share/

Related Post/Content Managers
A plugin with this functionality allows the audience to **find posts with similar content** to the one they are reading.

With this type of extension you improve your blog's dwell time and page views metrics. More content read increases the chances of conversion, that some of the promoted products are of interest, follow the affiliate link, buy and get your commission.

Recommended free extension: Yet Another Related Posts Plugin (YARPP). It is a plugin that displays posts related to the post the user is currently reading. Automatically added related posts can increase visits to your blog by over 10%.

Free download from: YARPP
https://es.wordpress.org/plugins/yet-another-related-posts-plugin/

WooCommerce
Plugin to convert your WordPress into an **e-commerce store**

WooCommerce is an open source, customizable e-commerce platform built for WordPress.

WooCommerce is a free plugin that allows you to create online stores in WordPress. It allows you to sell or promote as an affiliate all kinds of products and services.

You will need to install the woocommerce plugin if, for example, you participate in Amazon's affiliate program and want to promote the items in **store format.**

With **WooCommerce** you create your e-commerce website, you register the items, include descriptions and in the buy button you insert your affiliate link which will redirect the customer to Amazon, where they will buy the product and you will earn the commission. Very easy.

Free woocommerce download:
https://wordpress.org/plugins/woocommerce

Specific plugins for affiliate marketing
As our blog grows, we publish more and more valuable content, we recommend more products, in the same proportion we increase the number of affiliate links to our blog, pages, content, more and more of various aspects to manage...

This expansion of the content and the number of affiliate links on our blog makes it increasingly complicated to manage affiliate links.

Remember that affiliate links are the bridge between your website and that of the merchant who identifies you and assigns you the commission after the sale. The management of your affiliate links cannot fail, it has to be clean and perfect or there will be no commissions.

You need tools that help us and facilitate this task, such as:

[ThirstyAffiliates] This extension allows you to easily manage **affiliate links** in your posts.

With this plugin we have the option to **replace the keywords** we choose **for our affiliate link**, without having to do it manually and one by one. It saves time and avoids making mistakes.

Download free ThirstyAffiliates:
https://wordpress.org/plugins/thirstyaffiliates/

[Ad Inserter] Ad and affiliate link management add-on with many advanced advertising features for inserting ad codes and affiliate links.

This extension supports all types of ads, including Google AdSense, Google Ad Manager, contextual Amazon Native Shopping Ads, Media.net, **Info Links** and banners.

Free download of Ad Inserter:
https://wordpress.org/plugins/ad-inserter/

Regulatory compliance extension Cookie information and acceptance

Yes, that's right, my lawyer keeps insisting on the different legal aspects to be taken into account.

EU Cookie Law for GDPR/CCPA. EU Cookie Law is a lightweight and powerful solution to comply with EU Cookie Law, GDPR and CCPA, with pop-up windows and options to block scripts before acceptance.

Plugin that allows you to obtain the user's consent and acceptance of cookies on our website and thus **comply with European data protection regulations.**

The recommended extension is: It contains several customizations to perfectly fit your website and keep cookies under control (before and after consent). Simply install the plugin and follow the instructions on the settings page.

Download for free EU Cookie Law:
https://es.wordpress.org/plugins/eu-cookie-law

How to speed up your affiliate blog startup.

Do you want to speed up the launch of your blog and don't want to get into IT trouble? On fiverr.com a freelancer will do the job for you from $10, without your finances trembling.

$ $ $ $ $

The secret: 2 X 10

How to drive traffic to your affiliate links

Discover the 2 characteristics that your blog traffic must have to get 10,000 € per month.

To succeed in affiliate marketing you need to generate **a lot of quality traffic** to your affiliate links. Yes, yes, affiliate marketing, to a large extent, is a **numbers game, because you need to:**
- Numerous valuable and unique content
- Numerous traffic to your blog
- Numerous targeted traffic to the merchant's site from your affiliate links
- Numerous conversions
- Numerous commissions

Well, then, what is **quality traffic**, what **2 characteristics do** we need the **"numerous"** traffic to have in order to be considered as such? The two distinguishing features of **quality traffic** are:

1# Connection & Relevance
2# Purchasing power

1# Connection & Relevance

Not everything works. Just any user traffic will not do. They have to be users who connect with the content of the blog. Users who find your website and the products you promote relevant.

> *There is no point in attracting 100,000 users to your "Cat World" blog who happen to be allergic to felines.*
> *You have managed to get traffic but, you are not able to get conversions, nor commissions.*
> *"Bad business brother"*

In short, attract **relevant users**. Relevant users are those who show interest in your content and the products you promote. They love them. They love them.

2 # Purchasing power

They are potential customers **if they have the purchasing power to buy** the products you promote. They have money and can pay.

This group finds your advice useful, valuable and they have **the ability to buy**, they can purchase the products you promote on your affiliate marketing website.

Hypothesis

You launch the blog: luxurysportscars.com. You publish valuable, excellent, interesting content, but the audience of your website comes from developing countries with an average salary of **$100 per month, in this case, my friend**, you will hardly be able to monetize your website, they can not buy the products you promote.

You have an audience, there is traffic. They are interested in your content, but **your audience lacks purchasing power. Purchasing power.**

No conversions. No commissions. They are not relevant users for a blog that promotes products for owners of those brands (Ferrari, Lamborghini, Lotus...).

There will be connection, traffic, interest in your content, but there will be no conversions due to lack of purchasing power.

$ $ $ $ $

How to attract traffic to your affiliate links The 15 foolproof methods to get 15,000 free visits in 15 days

Traffic is just as important as customer traffic is to a physical store. No traffic. No sales. No business.
Game over.

The **15** most important **sources** within your reach to get **15,000** free traffic visits in **15 days** to your website and affiliate links are:

1. **Create valuable content.** Post published on the blog with relevant information for the community that follows you, this is what we call content marketing or Inbound Marketing.
2. **Do SEO.** Apply organic positioning strategies so that your valuable content appears in the first positions in Google.
3. **Write** as a guest on **blogs similar** to yours.
4. Leave **comments** on related blogs.
5. Share the content on **Social Networks.**
6. Include the address of your blog in your **email signature**
7. **Email marketing**. Create your list of subscribers and do email marketing on a regular basis.
8. Answer questions on **Quora.**
9. Record and broadcast videos on **YouTube**. In the description of each video include the domain of your blog and the links of the products you promote.
10. Live **Webinars**. Advertise your blog.
11. **Social networks.** Facebook, Instagram, Twitter..., in every post you share on social networks include your affiliate links.
12. In the **instant messaging** platform such as whatsapp or telegram that you use, advertise your blog and promote products among your contacts and groups.
13. Include the blog address and affiliate links in the content you create in **eBook** format, or in **PDF,** in **power point** presentations (...)
14. Maybe from your **podcasts**...
15. Participating in **forums**, Contribute valuable content and include your affiliate links.

Let's take a look at each of these powerful sources capable of providing free traffic to our website:

1.- Content of value. What it is and how to create it. To be or not to be

It's not about you. It's about them.

Principles that content must meet to be considered valuable in affiliate marketing:

#Be valuable. Be interesting

Content that solves your audience's problems is valuable and interesting. Nothing more. Nothing less.

This is the first big idea that you must anchor in your mind, if you want to be the owner of a successful affiliate marketing business capable of turning over **10.000€** every month.

When we talk about valuable content, we are referring to generating information that:
- Helping people
- Solve your problems
- It is a useful resource
- Make a difference
- Unique, only published on your blog

Make it different. Make it useful. Make it unique or **don't do it at all.**

#Beinteresting. Connect with your audience

Create topics that address the concerns and worries of your website's (relevant) audience.

Tool

An excellent tool in this regard is **Quora**. It is a platform that connects users who have concerns and **ask questions** with Internet users who contribute solutions and **provide answers.**

Research on Quora what **worries** your community and contribute the solution in your blog. Do it and you will be generating valuable content.

Let's see how to apply it. **Dog story.** Let's say you love dogs, you have a German Shepherd you adopted when he was a puppy.

You have decided to create the blog cachorrosfelices.com, you are going to create content based on your knowledge gained from your experience in breeding them. You are in a position to provide valuable advice.

You are going to monetize the blog with the following affiliate programs:
- zooplus.com
- Amazon Associates

You research on **Quora** what worries puppy owners, especially first timers, they are willing to pull the bank card with ease, in the same way that happens with "first time Homo Sapiens", everything is little when it comes to the first puppy, right? :)

You see that there is one issue that concerns most first-time puppy owners:

"How to train a puppy to relieve itself outside the home."

Voila, you have the first topic of general interest for your blog. We will continue to use Quora to detect what more topics interest and concern our audience and we will publish valuable content, able to provide solutions.

#Be viral
Ideally, your content should be disseminated through social networks and instant messaging applications (whatsapp, telegram...).

Making content viral means that your users, your community, and your audience's audience, spread your blog content, increase your reach, increase traffic to your website, at no cost. Free of charge. Free.

But what makes a post viral? Some distinctive features that trigger virality are content that...

- **Excite.** It is achieved by a sense of humor, intelligent, surprising, curious, innovative content?
  Tell stories that stimulate positive emotions and the chances of the content going viral skyrocket.
- **SEO optimized.** It complies with the SEO optimization rules. We will see them later. Interesting and well-optimized content makes it easier to appear in the first positions in Google. In this case, users click, read and share.
- **Impactful headline.** The title of your post makes a difference. Studies indicate that an attractive title makes 8 out of 10 Internet users click and continue reading.
- **Opinion leader.** When your community considers you an opinion leader, they give credibility to all your advice, that's what it means to be considered an expert in the field. At this point it is easy for them to share your content on their favorite social network.

Sergio Ramos vs. Sergio Tramos

When Sergio Ramos **(famous European soccer player)** publishes content on his twitter account, where he has hundreds of thousands of followers, the chances of being retweeted are higher than if the same content is shared by **Sergio Tramos** who has a dozen followers and is far from being an opinion leader.

Once again, we can see that to generate traffic and viralize content, to a large extent, it is still a question of numbers and size.

Hundreds of thousands of **Sergio Ramos fans**, compared to dozens of **Sergio Tramos** fans, there's no color...
SIZE, in this case, DOES MATTER :)

- **Number of words. Length. Size matters here too.** Studies show that articles with useful content, and with a length of around **2,000 words** spread more.

Why? The reason is because a well-written, problem-solving, 2,000-word piece of content provides enough useful information that it deserves to be known to your audience's network, which is why we decided to share it.

The effort, in this case, is rewarded in the form of retweets.

Finally, create a publication calendar. Plan. Make an effort, elaborate a publication schedule, decide how often your content will be published. Create the calendar and transmit it to your community.

Case Study

The article: *"The best dog food",* published on the blog lomejorparamican.com, has been **shared 83 times** on **Facebook at the time** of writing.

By the way, this website monetizes with Amazon Associates.

2.- Organic positioning. Do SEO

It's not enough to create valuable content. You have to have an SEO strategy so that your publications appear in the first positions in Google.

The main factors affecting search engine positioning are:
- **Blog loading time.** Blogs that take a long time to load are penalized by Google's algorithm and their content is ranked lower.
  You have at your disposal free plugins, tools that optimize the loading times of your WordPress. The goal is that your blog loads in less than a second.
- **Ease of navigation.** The content of the blog must be well structured and easy to find.
- **Quality,** interesting, relevant and **unique content.** Copy-paste does not rank on Google.
- **Rich in keywords.** Make a study of **"Keywords",** of Keywords.

Find out what your audience searches for on google. Use SEO keyword analysis tools such as Google Keyword Planner from Adwords or Keyword Surfer, it will be useful to find out:
- **Volume** of searches for each term.
- **Competitiveness**. What are your chances of positioning your content in the first results in Google (low competition) or the opposite in case of high competition (difficult to appear in the first search results).
- They provide similar terms.

- **Keyword density.** Your blog content has to be rich in the keywords you want to rank for but without going overboard.
The number of keywords must represent a maximum of **5%** of the total text, above this percentage Google can penalize you as a spammer and stop appearing in the search results.
- The **title and subtitle** must **contain** the keywords you want to rank for.
- Insert **internal links** in your posts. Internal links provide value to your audience and make it easier for Google to index the content.
Making life easy for Google spiders is good business for you, because it increases the chances of seeing your content in the first places.
- **Optimize images.** In the posts you have to insert images, they attract users and generate traffic, but if they are heavy, the blog takes time to load and Google penalizes. Use plugins that compress images and weigh less.

    A free plugin that serves this purpose is: **Smush - Lazy Load Images, Optimize & Compress Images.**
    Download it for free **at:**
    https://es.wordpress.org/plugins/wp-smushit/
- **Publish regularly.** Google prioritizes recent and updated content. Tips:
    - Create an editorial calendar
    - Public on a regular basis
    - Launch the posts on the same day and time, create expectation, so that your community waits impatiently

for the new publication. For example, every Wednesday at 8:00, so they can read while traveling to work by public transport.
    - Update the content. Make a renovation plan. Give your old content a facelift.
- **Responsive design.** 80% of the traffic to a blog comes from mobile devices. Most WordPress templates are responsive, that is, they are designed to adapt to all mobile devices: desktop, tablets and smartphones.

3.- Write as a guest in blogs of similar subject matter to ours.
Guest posting on someone else's blog with similar content to ours is an excellent way to get free traffic, for the following reasons:
- We access a **similar community.** If the blog has a similar theme to ours, it means that its community shares the same interests and, they may end up landing on our blog, following the links we have included in our publication.
  With a well-written and useful article we can awaken their interest and help them discover the valuable content of our website.
  Remember to **insert links** pointing to your website, this way you will get free, quality traffic and improve your backlink.
  Links to our blog, backlink strategy, improves our **SEO positioning.**
- Writing in a blog that is a reference in the sector makes it easier to be recognized as an **opinion leader.**
- **You increase your list of subscribers,** because you can get their email addresses and increase your list of newsletter subscribers.

Writing as a guest on a quality blog and well positioned in Google, increases the visibility of our website.
Improve organic positioning.
It makes it easier for us to be recognized as opinion leaders and allows us to obtain subscribers to our newsletter.

4.- Leave comments on related blogs

Writing valuable, well-crafted reviews that provide useful information on quality blogs with related content and including links that point to our website is another easy and free way to get traffic from an audience similar to ours.

5.- Share the content on social networks

Sharing your blog posts on social networks: Facebook, Twitter, Instagram, Pinterest, LinkedIn, is another way to get noticed and get visitors.

Use a tool like **hootsuite** to plan and automate content publishing:
- When (day and time)
- Where to publish the post (in which social network or networks)

Include buttons on your blog to make it easy for visitors to share posts on social networks and instant messaging applications.

6.- Sign all your emails

Configure your email manager so that your blog address appears in the signature of all your emails.

You can also include a call to action such as: (enter subscribe and get the free ebook....). This is a simple action and at no cost to you.

"If you add a little to the little and do it that way often, it will soon become a lot."

Hesiod

7.- Email marketing. Transform your audience into a community.
The biggest and best asset of your affiliate marketing business is your subscriber list.

This list allows you to have the initiative to communicate with your community, whenever you want. Create your subscriber list and you will own your website's audience.

Relying on social networks as a communication channel with your community is a danger and a risk.

In this situation, the community belongs to the social network, it is not yours. You have permission to communicate with your audience through them, but if that network goes out of fashion or users migrate to a new one that is a hit... Bye bye community, because it was not your property, it was borrowed. You had it rented.

On the other hand, if you have the email addresses of your users, you will be able to contact them whenever you want. You will go from being a renter to an owner.

Install in WordPress an extension to capture emails from your community, from your users. **Encourage** subscribers to sign up to your subscriber list, as the Romans would say, make...

Quid pro quo.
Something for something

Exchange the email for an ebook, or for participating in a webinar, or in a sweepstakes..., whatever you can think of. The more valuable and appealing the gift, the more contacts you will get.

Long live barter!

The more valuable the user perceives the gift to be, the more email addresses you will collect.

Don't be tiresome

Don't exhaust your community with daily shipments

Avoid using language close to collegiality.

Anecdote

There are "alleged gurus", shamans of the "Everything at 100" on these topics (affiliation, digital nomadism, infoproducts...,) that I sometimes follow, I am subscribed to their mailing list as a "curious anthropologist".

From time to time I browse through their emails, especially if I'm looking for a laugh and want to relax. It is amazing how concerned they are about my well being, they send (chase) me with **daily emails, yes, yes every day** and I read them again and again....

> *... Jack, I'm worried about you... ...I can't sleep thinking...*
> *Jack by God, Buddha and Jehovah, do not miss this unique, unrepeatable opportunity...*
> *... Jack, please, please, s'il vous...*

Do they sound credible, sincere, perhaps artificial? In my opinion they are tiresome, very tiresome and heavy?

Three tips to finish this section on email marketing:
- A. **Don't exhaust** your community. Don't flood your users' inbox with emails, because they will label you as a spammer.
- B. **Be sincere.** It is not sincere who is suddenly extremely concerned about my welfare and future. All this without knowing each other at all.
- C. Manage your email list with a powerful email marketing platform such as: **Convertkit.**

8.- Answer questions on Quora

Earlier we talked about Quora, the platform that mediates between audiences with questions and users who provide answers, to find out what worries your audience and write content as a solution.

Now I propose you to use **Quora** to answer questions and concerns raised on that platform on topics similar to the content and products promoted on your website.

Insert in your answers a link with the domain of your online site, Quora readers will recognize you as an expert on the subject and will end up clicking on the link and browsing your blog. More free traffic to your website.

9.- Videos on YouTube

Create a YouTube channel on the topic of your blog and in the description of each video include affiliate links and the address of your blog.

10.- Live Webinars

Broadcast live webinars to show the benefits of the product you are promoting, take advantage of it and spread the address of your blog.

11.- Social networks. Facebook, Instagram, Twitter... Share the content on your favorite social networks.

12.- Instant messaging platform such as whatsapp or telegram

Create user groups on the instant messaging platform you use regularly and share content and information about the products you promote.

13.- Include affiliate links in all the material you create, whatever the format, eBook, PDF, power point, infographics, always include your affiliate links to your website and newsletter subscription.

14.- Podcast...

If you consider podcasts as an ideal channel to promote products, remember to record in each episode information about your affiliate business, name of the website, where to go, more published content and how to subscribe to your newsletter.

15.- Participate in forums

Another option is to participate in forums on similar topics, helping the members of that community with information that helps to solve their problems, concerns and providing useful information in general. To these 15 sources, add any other that you consider useful for this purpose.

$ $ $ $ $

Blogs that fail. The three most frequent and stupid mistakes they make. How to avoid them

The three most serious and common mistakes that novice marketers and lazy bloggers make are:
1. Filling the blog with banners
2. Copy and paste promotional content
3. Overdose of praise

Let's review this hat-trick of **"Homo Bloggers nada Sapiens"**:

1.- Banners do not convert.
We Internet users have developed a whole new skill: **banner blindness**, we ignore them, we ignore them, we ignore them, we ignore them.

A strategy to monetize an affiliate blog based on plaguing our website with advertising banners is doomed to failure. Affiliate links that are **wisely inserted** along useful, relevant and unique content convert at a higher rate.

2.- Copy and paste promotional content
When the content strategy is based on a copy-paste of descriptions collected on the web, the marketer wastes time.

It is irrelevant content, it does not help users, it does not create community and it is difficult to be positioned in search engines. With this strategy we proclaim...

> *-Hey, don't come back here. You're going to read more of the same stuff you find on every other blog. Nothing new...*

In short, copy and paste does not position in Google. You will not get organic traffic, the blogger who acts like this, if he wants to get commissions, will have to buy traffic, invest in advertising, because he will not get it by positioning (organic).

The professional who aspires to a healthy affiliate marketing business model has to generate quality and unique content.
You can't base your content strategy on more of the same.

3.- Overdose of praise

"You can fool everybody some of the time. You can fool some of the people all the time. But you can't fool everybody all the time."

Abraham Lincoln

The greatest asset of a successful affiliate marketer is his credibility. The community must appreciate honesty in all your opinions and recommendations.

You have to be **credible** to your users. When you do this it is easier to get them to follow your affiliate links, send traffic to the merchant's site, lead to conversions and earn your commissions. Choose which side of the court you prefer to play on:

You are credible. You will be listened to. There will be conversions, commissions and money to your bank account. Your content will be viral, more traffic, more conversions...

They do not perceive sincerity in your proposals. There will be no conversions, no commissions and your bank account will continue to acquire a worrying reddish hue.

$ $ $ $ $

Part 5. Best affiliate programs for beginners

Discover the 20 best affiliate programs for beginners who want to go from €0 to €10,000 per month

The **20 excellent programs** to get started in the world of affiliate marketing are:
1. Amazon Associates
2. ClickBank
3. Hotmart
4. Siteground
5. Bluehost
6. Kinsta
7. Namecheap
8. Long Tail Pro
9. Short Pixel
10. Fiverr
11. Udemy
12. Coursera
13. Canva
14. Hostgator
15. EBay Partner Network
16. Teachable
17. Printful
18. Adultfrienfinder.com
19. Aliexpress
20. Booking

Note. The estimation of visits is made with the similarsites.com application.

1. Amazon Associates

Amazon Associates is Amazon's affiliate program. It is probably the largest affiliate program in existence. Amazon helps content creators, webmasters, publishers and bloggers monetize their traffic.

Let's review the figures of this digital commerce colossus. They are impressive. Highlights:
- 2020 Turnover: US$ **386 billion**
- Net income: US$21.**33** billion
- Worldwide workforce: 1.3 million employees
- **400** million products for sale in its catalog and growing in both products and categories.

Monthly traffic of visits to your websites:
- Amazon.com: **2** billion visits per month
- Amazon.es: **150** million monthly visits
- Amazon.co.uk: **286** million visits per month

As an affiliate you can take advantage of this online sales empire thanks to its affiliate program: **Amazon Associates.**

Amazon offers more than **400 million products** and various programs available. Associates (affiliates) have tools to create links that direct their audience to Amazon's website and earn money through commissions paid.

Table of **commissions** paid by **Amazon Associates**

Product categories	Standard commission income
	Direct Purchases
Amazon Fashion	10 %
Clothing, shoes, jewelry, watches, luggage, Amazon private label fashion (women's, men's, children's)	12 %
Handmade	10 %
Home Furniture, do-it-yourself, home,	7 %

kitchen and dining, patio, lawn and garden, power and hand tools	8 %
Consumables	6 %
Beer, wine and spirits, food, baby pet products, beauty, health and personal care, personal care appliances, stationery and office supplies	7 %
Digital & media	6 %
Books, ebooks for Kindle, music, DVD and Blu-ray, digital video games, software, digital software, digital music, digital video	7 %
Hobbies and Car	6 %
Outdoor leisure, toys and games, sports and fitness, musical instruments, cars and motorcycles, business and industry products	7 %
Amazon Devices	3 %
Fire TV, Kindle and Echo devices and accessories	4 %
Electronics and IT	3 %
Computers, electronics, photography, major household appliances, home entertainment, smartphones and mobile telephony, video games	4 %
Video game consoles	1 %
Other categories (except gift vouchers)	3 %
Prime Wardrobe purchases, gift certificates	0 %

What is meant by "Direct Assigned Purchase" and "Indirect Assigned Purchase"?

Direct Subscription Purchase. An Affiliated Purchase of a Product that belongs to the same Product Category as the product detail page accessed through the "Special Link" that gave rise to such Affiliated Purchase.

Indirect Referral Purchase. The Referral Purchase of a Product that is in a Product Category other than the Product detail page accessed from the "Special Link" that triggered the Referral Purchase. Amazon Associates pays 1.5% for this item, except for video game consoles (1%), Prime Wardrobe purchases and gift certificates (0%).

Subscribe to Amazon Associates:
https://affiliate-program.amazon.com/

2. ClickBank

ClickBank is an e-commerce retailer of **digital products.** Estimated monthly traffic: **400,000** visits. Highlights:

- Clickbank sells infoproducts (digital products) that are marketed through its affiliate network.
- In short, ClickBank is a Marketplace, a meeting point between creators of infoproducts (ebooks, video courses, audiobooks...) and the affiliates in charge of promoting and publicizing this digital content.
- Type of products for sale in ClickBank:
    - Courses
    - Ebooks
    - Software
    - Training programs
    - Methods
    - Audiobooks
- Categories collected in ClickBank:
    - Art and entertainment
    - Products promoted on television
    - E-Business & E-Marketing
    - Games
    - Health & Fitness
    - Home & Garden
    - Languages
    - Parenting & Family
    - Self-help
    - Spirituality, New Age and Alternative Beliefs

ClickBank **figures:**
1. **4,000** digital products for sale in the Marketplace.
2. **4.2** billion in commissions paid to affiliates.
3. **220** million customers in 190 countries.

The **commission** that affiliates can earn can be up to **90%.**
Join the ClickBank affiliate program:
https://accounts.clickbank.com/master/makebank.html

3. Hotmart

Hotmart is a Marketplace for the sale and distribution of digital products.

Estimated monthly traffic for hotmart.com: **62,000,000** monthly visits. On its web site, hotmail describes itself as a
distance learning platform focused on Latin America.

It is the largest and most complete distance learning platform in Latin America, with:
- **420,000** registered **products**
- **29 million** users
- Sales in **188 countries**

Hotmart's platform facilitates the distribution of digital products, provides hosting services for these products, tools to assist in their sale, process payments for these sales and distribute the value to the parties involved (content producers and affiliates) in an automated manner. **Hotmart** is, to a large extent, the Latin equivalent of ClickBank.

Types of digital products or infoproducts that are marketed in Hotmart:
- Ebooks PDF or EPUB
- Audiobooks, podcasts and music (mp3, wma);
- Video lessons
- Lectures and screencasts (MPEG, FLV, MOV, WMV)
- Software
- Images
- Scripts and any other file format that can be downloaded over the Internet
- Subscriptions that allow affiliates and producers to earn recurring commissions...

The **commission** paid to the affiliate can exceed **80%**.

Subscribe to Hotmart's affiliate program: https://hotmart.com/en

4. Siteground

SiteGround is a web hosting company, currently has two million domains registered worldwide.

Estimated monthly traffic: **26,000** visits. Services provided by siteground.es:
- Shared accommodation
- Cloud hosting
- Enterprise Solutions
- E-mail managers
- Domain registration

Features of Siteground's affiliate program:
- **Commissions paid.** There is an escalation depending on the number of monthly sales:
    - 1-5 Sales /month 40€ /sale
    - 6-10 Sales /month 60€ /sale
    - 11-20 Sales /month 75€ /sale
    - 21+ Sales /month Customized commissions
- Weekly payments
- No minimum payment limits
  Join the affiliate program: https://www.siteground.com

5. Bluehost

Bluehost is one of the most popular web hosting companies.
- It currently has more than 2,000,000 sites hosted on its servers.
- Estimated number of monthly visits: **796,000**

Bluehost markets and provides:
- WordPress Hosting
- Hosting
    - Shared accommodation
    - Dedicated hosting
    - VPS Hosting
- Domains
- Online Store
- Professional Services
    - SEO. Organic positioning
    - SEM. Pay per click advertising. PPC
- E-mail address

Commissions paid in the affiliate program:
- 65 for each hosting sale

Bluehost pays the commission 45 days after the purchase. Payment is processed between the 16th and the last day of the month. The affiliate must have a minimum balance of $100 in order for the payment to be released.

Subscribe to the affiliate program:
https://www.bluehost.com/affiliates

6. Kinsta

Hosting company specialized in quality managed **WordPress**. Estimated monthly traffic: 3,**970,000** visits.

Kinsta hosting features:
- Fully managed
- Secure hosting, as secure as Fort Knox is secure
- Free migrations
- Maximum download speed superior to its competitors
- Daily backups
- Google Cloud Platform

Kinsta Affiliate Program:
- You can earn up to **$500** for each referred customer who signs up for a hosting plan.
- **10%** monthly **recurring** commission forever. For life.

Join the Kinsta affiliate program: https://affiliate.kinsta.com/register

7. Namecheap

Namecheap is an ICANN accredited domain name registrar. It provides domain registration and web hosting. Estimated monthly traffic: 2,**000,000 visits.**

Namecheap in figures:
- 11 million users
- 10 million domain name registrations
  Services provided by Namecheap:
- Domain registration
- Hosting
- Specialized WordPress hosting
- E-mail services
- Security

Namecheap affiliate program **features. Commissions:**

Product	Commissions
Domains (registrations / transfers)	20%
Hosting Packages (Stellar, Reseller, VPS and Dedicated Servers)	35%
SSL Certificates	35%

Private e-mail	20%
Premium DNS	20%

VPN

Free monthly trial	2 * per registration and 40% for up to 9 months
1-year plan and 3-year plan	50%

Source: https://www.namecheap.com/commission-rates
Join Namecheap's affiliate program:
https://www.namecheap.com/affiliates/

8. Long Tail Pro

Long Tail Pro is a long **tail** keyword research tool. It facilitates the work of organic positioning (SEO). Estimated monthly traffic: **15,000** visits

Long Tail Pro helps to find thousands of long tail keywords, makes it easier to implement SEO techniques, because it allows to find out what relevant content to create based on those long tail keywords provided by this tool.

These are less competitive keywords that can bring you thousands of visits to your blog.

Commission rate offered: 30% of all sales on a **recurring basis.** Lifetime.

Become a Long Tail Pro affiliate:

https://longtailpro.com/become-an-affiliate-of-long-tail-pro/#become-an-affiliate

9. Short Pixel

It is a tool to compress and optimize images so that they weigh less. Estimated monthly traffic: **10,000** visits. The benefits of using Short Pixel are:
- Increase the loading speed of the web.
- Improve the SEO ranking of the site.

Commission rate: **30% recurring,** month to month. Lifetime

Sign up for the Short Pixel affiliate program:

https://shortpixel.com/free-sign-up-affiliate

10. Fiverr

Fiverr is a marketplace for digital services. Freelancers offer their services to clients from all over the world through this platform:

    Estimated monthly traffic of:
- fiverr.com: 2,750,000 visits (Global)
- en.fiverr.com: 76,000 visits (Spain)
- Fiverr has more than **300 categories.**
- In 2020, **it had a turnover of 107 million dollars.**

Commission rate.

The commission ranges from $15 to $150 USD on the user's first purchase of a product on Fiverr. Depending on the category of the product you will receive:

$ 150
- All Fiverr Pro services

$ 50
- Industrial and product design.
- Graphics and Design
- Data science
- Data
- Mobile applications
- Programming and technology
- E-commerce development
- Programming and technology

$ 40
- Website builders and CMS
- Programming and technology
- Videos with lyrics and music
- Video and animation
- Web programming
- Programming and technology
- Data processing
- Data
- Architecture and Interior Design
- Graphic design
- Game development
- Programming and technology
- Web and mobile design
- Graphic design

$ 30
- Logo creator
- SEO
- Digital advertising
- T-shirts and merchandise
- Graphic design
- Research and summaries
- Writing and translation
- Job consultation
- Business
- Proofreading and editing
- Writing and translation
- Financial consultation
- Business
- Producers and composers
- Music and audio

$ 25
- Illustration
- Graphic design
- Gambling
- Lifestyle
- Articles and blog posts
- Writing and translation
- Video marketing
- Digital advertising
- Social media marketing
- Digital advertising
- Resume writing
- Writing and translation
- Narration
- Music and audio
- Short video ads
- Video and animation

$ 15
- Other categories not covered

✓ Fiverr Business: **$ 100 + 10%** for 12 months
✓ Fiverr Affiliates: **10%** of each referred affiliate's earnings for their entire lifetime

✓ Learn from Fiverr: **30%** for each course sale

Join the Fiverr affiliate program:
https://www.fiverr.com/affiliates/signup

11. Udemy

Udemy is an online learning and teaching platform with:
- **155,000** courses
- **40** million students
- Estimated monthly traffic: **110,000,000** visits

Udemy provides tools for users to create a course, promote it and earn money from the registration fees paid by students.

The commission rate paid by Udemy is **15%**. When the affiliate's sales exceed $5,000 per month, the percentage paid is increased.

Udemy affiliate program registration:
https://affiliatesupport.udemy.com/hc/es/articles

12. Coursera

Marketplace with online courses from more than 200 universities and prestigious companies such as Google and IBM. Estimated monthly traffic: 9**,000,000** visits.

Coursera in figures:
- 75 million individually enrolled students
- Employees of more than 100 Fortune 500 companies use its courses.
- More than 6,400 campuses, businesses and governments come to Coursera to access their online training.

Affiliation program **features:**
- Commission rate for affiliates: between **10%** and **45% of CPA**
- Cookie Duration: **30 days**

Subscription to the Coursera affiliate program:
https://app.partnersmy.com/affiliates/signup.php#SignupForm

13. Canva

The best online design website. Canva is a software with a set of graphic design tools. It uses a drag and drop format.

Canva in figures:
- Provides access to more than 60 million photographs.
- 5 million vectors, graphics and fonts.
- Estimated monthly traffic: **9,500,000** visits
- Canva has 15 million users from 190 countries.

It is easy to use and quick to learn. Used by professionals and amateurs of graphic design.

Canva Affiliate Program. Commissions paid:
- They pay up to **$36** for each user who subscribes to Canva Pro
- Recurring payment options are available.

Subscribe to the canva affiliate program:
https://app.impact.com/campaign-promo-signup/Canva.brand?execution=e1s1

14. Hostgator

Hostgator is a provider of:
- Shared, reseller, VPS and dedicated hosting
- Domain registration
- Website builder

Estimated monthly traffic: **225,000** visits

Commission rates paid:
- 1-5 sales: 65 $ / subscription
- 6-10 sales: 75 $ / subscription
- 11-20 sales: 100 $ / subscription
- 21 + sales: $125/description

The affiliate who achieves 21 subscriptions in a month earns an income of **$2,625,** not bad at all.

Subscription to Hostgator's affiliate program:
https://www.hostgator.com/affiliates

15. EBay Partner Network

Ebay is an auction and e-commerce platform. Estimated monthly traffic:
- ebay.com **176,000,000** hits
- ebay.com 9,**350,000** hits

A wide variety of products and services can be transacted on ebay, such as items from:
- Technology
- Engine
- Collecting
- Fashion
- Baby boy
- House and garden
- Sports
- Pet supplies
- Industrial equipment...

On eBay you can find new and second-hand products, buy outright or in an auction if your bid is the highest.

eBay figures:
- 1.4 billion items for sale
- 80% of the items are new
- 183 million buyers
- Works in 190 markets
- 90% if the items are in the category: "Buy it now".

Commissions paid by eBay. The commissions paid by eBay for each sale start at 1% (real estate) up to 4% (spare parts and accessories. Fashion).

You can see what corresponds to each category in the attached table and download the PDF in the following link:

Tabla de tasas

Categorías	Subcategorías	% de ventas	Cap (USD)
Empresas e industria	Empresas e industria	2.5%	$225
Artículos para coleccionar	Arte y antigüedades; Billetes y monedas; Artesanía; Muñecas y peluches; Coleccionables varios; Sellos; Juguetes, juegos y aficiones; Artículos del mundo del espectáculo; Deportes y ocio; Cerámica y cristal	3.0%	$550
Electrónica	Cámaras y fotografía; Móviles y accesorios; Televisión, imagen y sonido; Videojuegos y consolas	2.0%	$550
	Ordenadores/Tabletas y operación en red	1.5%	$550
Moda	Ropa, zapatos y accesorios; Salud y belleza; Joyería y relojes	4.0%	$550
Casa y Jardín	Bebidas alcohólicas y alimentación, Bebé, Casa y jardín varios, Electrodomésticos, Artículos para mascotas	3.0%	$550
Estilo de vida	Tarjetas regalo y cupones, Estilo de vida varios, Instrumentos musicales, Entradas y eventos, Deporte	3.0%	$550
Medios de difusión	Libros, cómics y revistas; DVD y películas; Música	3.0%	$550
Recambios y accesorios	eBay Motor	4.0%	$100
	Recambios y accesorios de vehículos	3.0%	$550
Inmobiliaria	Inmobiliaria	1.0%	$100
Otras	Otras	4.0%	$550

https://partnernetwork.ebay.es/page/rate-card

Subscribe to the eBay affiliate program:
https://partnernetwork.ebay.es/

16. Teachable

Teachable is a SAAS (Software As A Service) e-learning platform for creating and selling online courses, coaching services and subscriptions. Estimated monthly traffic: **372,000 visits.**

Affiliate program **features:**
- **From 30% to 50%** commission, depending on the number of affiliate conversions.
- Recurring commissions: **30%** (on subscriptions to coaching or mentoring programs)
- Duration of cookies: **90 days**

Enrollment in the affiliate program: https://teachable.com/partners

17. Printful

Printful is the world leader in **print-on-demand and** dropshipping services that allow you to scale brands and businesses without investing in inventory. Expected monthly traffic: **445,000** visits

Printful helps people turn their ideas into brands and products.

Categories of products that the entrepreneur can design, sell and Printful can make and ship to customers are:
- Men's clothing
- Women's clothing
- Clothing for children and teenagers
- Caps and hats
- Men's clothing
- Women's clothing
- Clothing for children and teenagers
- Caps and hats
- Accessories
- Bags
- Backpacks
- Bum bags
- Cell phone cases
- Home Decoration
- Collections

- Brands
- All T-shirts
- T-shirts
- All over T-shirts
- T-shirts
- Crop tops
- Embroidered T-shirts
- Half sleeve T-shirts
- Long sleeve T-shirts
- All sweatshirts
- Hooded sweatshirts
- Sweatshirts
- Jackets
- Pants
- Sweat pants
- Leggins
- Skirts
- Shorts
- Dresses
- Swimsuits
- Sports bras
- Home Decoration
- T-shirts
- All over T-shirts
- T-shirts
- Crop tops
- Embroidered T-shirts
- Half sleeve T-shirts
- Long sleeve T-shirts
- Hooded sweatshirts
- Sweatshirts
- Jackets
- Pants
- Sweat pants
- Leggins
- Skirts
- Shorts
- Dresses
- Swimsuits

- Sports bras

(...)

Commission rate: **10%** of all orders placed by submitted customers and for **9 months.**

Affiliate program registration:
https://www.printful.com/es/auth/register

18. adultfriendfinder.com

adultfriender.com is an adult dating site. It is a swingers community.

adultfriendfinder.com in **figures:**
- 98,897,765 Sexy pictures
- 3,179,583 Connections
- Estimated monthly traffic: **1,140,000** visits

Affiliation program **features:**
- Commission of **up to 75%** on initial subscriptions and up to **55%** on recurring orders.
- Commissions are paid on a **weekly basis.**

Affiliate program subscription:
https://secure.adultfriendfinder.com/p/partners/affiliates

19. Aliexpress

AliExpress is an ecommerce, a marketplace, a communication platform between sellers and buyers. Founded in 2010 in China. It belongs to the Alibaba group. Estimated monthly traffic of aliexpress.com: 464,**000,000** visits.

Aliexpress offers the following services:
- Consumer sales
- Cloud computing
- Means of payment

Awin, affiliate platform provides the following information: **Commission rates collected in its affiliate program (2021) from the:**

6,92%
All products except electronics, including: women's clothing / men's clothing / children's clothing / accessories / cell phone accessories / indoor accessories / garden supplies

2,3%
Electronics: including cell phones / computer peripherals / tablets / desktops / laptops / home audio / video equipment / external storage / internal storage

5,38%
Other categories

On average, Aliexpress has very high **conversion rates for affiliates**, between **25% and 30%**. It means that a high amount of the traffic directed to booking makes a booking on their platform and, the affiliate gets their commission.

As a negative aspect of this affiliate program is that the **maximum commission** they pay is **33 € per sale**. The Amazon Associates affiliate program, on the other hand, does not have this restriction.

Enrollment in the Aliexpress affiliate program:
- Awin: https://ui.awin.com/publisher-signup/es/awin/step1
- Directly on aliexpress.com: https://portals.aliexpress.com/

20. Booking

Booking.com makes it easy for millions of travelers to live unique experiences. Booking provides a variety of transportation and accommodation options.

Estimated monthly traffic for booking.com: **145,000,000** visitors

Booking is a travel platform. It brings together established brands (Meliá, NH, Novotel...) and entrepreneurs of all sizes (owner-occupied apartments).

Booking.com is available in 43 languages and offers more than 28 million accommodation options, including more than 6.2 million choices in homes, apartments and other unique accommodations.

Booking in figures:
- 29,475,748 of rooms
- 2,563,380 of accommodations
- 1,550,000 nights booked each day

Source: https://www.booking.com/content/about.es.html

Main **features** of your affiliate program:
- Commission rates of the booking.com affiliate program.

No. reservations / month	% Affiliated Revenues
0-50	25%
51/150	30%
151-500	35%
501+	40%

Source: https://affiliates-support.booking.com

- Cookie duration: 24 hours

Booking affiliate program registration:
https://www.booking.com

$ $ $ $ $

Part 6. Examples of affiliate websites

25 best affiliate marketing websites. Number 15 will amaze you. Get inspired!

In this chapter we will look at and analyze **25 websites** that monetize through affiliate marketing.

These 25 websites should be a source of inspiration for you. Observe and analyze the following aspects:
- What they do
- How they do it
- What category or categories do you work in?
- What niche or niches are targeted
- Do they express a sub-niche?
- Do you focus your efforts on a micro niche?
- What your content is based on: reviews, comparisons, articles, listings...

Once you have seen the 25 examples, make your own decisions, go your own way, test, practice, make mistakes, learn, make mistakes fast and make better mistakes.

There are websites from the United States while others are located in Spain, if you are not fluent in a language, install the Chrome translation extension.

Chrome extension:
https://play.google.com/store/apps/traductor

Let's take a look at these 25 websites that use affiliate marketing to earn revenue. Enjoy the journey...

1. www.dealnews.com

They offer daily to their community the best offers and coupons detected by their team of experts. Estimated monthly visits: **7.000.000**

This website is a search engine for products and offers in the following categories:

- Home and garden
- Clothing and accessories
- Health
- Beauty
- Electronics
- Computing
- Sports
- Financial Services
- Gifts
- Games and toys
- Gift card
- Movies, music and books
- Office supplies
- Home automation
- Outlet sales
- Travel
- Entertainment
- Automobile

www.dealnews.com is affiliated and works with the following **affiliate programs:**

1. Amazon
2. Home Depot
3. EBay
4. Macy's
5. Sam's Club
6. Kohl's
7. Wayfair

By collaborating with seven affiliate programs, you can offer users a variety of great products, prices and offers, so they can choose where to shop.

Key idea
Consider working on your affiliate website with various programs, like the people at dealnews.com do.

They also monetize web traffic through the Google Adsense advertising program, but that's another story.

At the time of writing this book they have over **5,000** products listed on their website. That's 5,000 hooks in the big web to try to catch good commissions.

Let's make the following hypothesis of possible income, let's suppose that these circumstances occur...
- 7,000,000 monthly traffic
- Divided by 5,000 products analyzed on the website
- This means that, on average, each article receives **1,400** visits per month.
- Assume a conversion rate of 3% = **42** sales per month.
- Commission per sale= 5 dollars
  5,000 products x 42 sales (3%) x $5 = $1,050,000 affiliate revenue

Type of promotional **content** published on the website:
On their blog they publish buying guides, tips to help customers improve their online shopping experience and acquire the skills to know how to get the best products at the best price. Examples
- How to obtain a refund from Amazon for late delivery
- The best offers for DIY tools
- The 5 best mattresses for babies

2. www.thisiswhyimbroke.com

thisiswhyimbroke.com is a website to find unique and wonderful gift ideas.
Estimated monthly visits: 1.**000.000**

This website stands out for its fun and funny product descriptions, for offering its community a catalog of unique, exclusive and fun items.
The design of this website aims to facilitate usability. It is very easy to navigate through the different categories.

They build their success through their clever product descriptions, a catalog full of unique items, the design of the site and how easy it is to browse. It entertains visitors and keeps them coming back again and again. You've built loyalty. Take note.

On this website they offer gift listings for every **occasion:**

- Father's Day
- Mother's Day
- Valentine's Day gifts for her
- Valentine's Day Gifts for the
- Anniversary for her
- Anniversary for
- Birthday gifts for the
- Christmas gifts
- Gifts for graduation
- Gifts in a wedding petition
- Gifts to groomsmen
- Bridesmaids' gifts

They also classify gifts by **category**:
- Enjoy a **unique experience:**
    - Enjoy a night in an underwater hotel, or in an igloo at the North Pole.
    - Cooking class with a famous and televised Top Chef.
- **Personalized** gifts
- Work **from home**
- **Funny. Funny**
- **Geek** world
- Passionate about series such as **Star Wars, Star Trek** and **Galactica.**
- **Harry Potter** World
- **Travel** accessory
- Camping and **outdoor**
- Survival and **Apocalypse...**

Gifts per **recipient:**
- Man
- Women
- Father
- Mother
- Children
- Teenage boys
- Teenage girls
- Couples
- Boyfriend
- Bride

- Husband
- Wife
- Father and mother
- Workmates

3. www.buzzfeed.com

BuzzFeed is an American digital media company focused on tracking viral content. Estimated monthly visits: **125.000.000**

It was founded on November 1, 2006, in New York City by Jonah Peretti and John S. Johnson III.

The firm describes itself as a "news and social entertainment company" with a focus on digital media and digital technology in order to provide the most compatible breaking news, original reporting, entertainment and video."

Buzzfeed is current information, breaking news, has contests, videos, incorporates recipes, crafts, ingenious DIY ideas, recycling, pets, business, social networks and also reports on trends.

One of the ways to monetize the 125 million users that visit their website every month is through affiliate marketing, by reviewing thousands of products that bring value to their community.

Example of promotional content:
- 55 mind-blowing science toys that kids and adults will love
- 51 incredible gifts for nature lovers. Recommended by true explorers, hikers and outdoor enthusiasts.
- 33 gifts for car lovers that will get their engines revving
- 37 products if your bedroom has virtually zero storage space

4. https://bestreviews.com

BestReviews is the place to go when you're about to buy something.

From heating blankets to trampolines to cordless drills, compare the best products from thousands of categories to provide the most trusted buying advice. Estimated monthly visits: **7,000,000**

BestReviews is owned by Tribune Publishing (NASDAQ: TPCO). BestReviews partners with multiple Tribune Publishing brands to bring product recommendations to consumers and earn commissions on sales.

Their website indicates:
Check out our reviews before you buy anything. We help ensure that you never end up with something mediocre. We make finding the best products fast and easy. Our experts research and test the things you're buying, then recommend the ones that best fit your needs and budget."
"Our goal is to make it easy to choose the best product and for the user to be confident in their purchasing decision."
www.bestreviews.com/about-us

BestReviews spends thousands of hours researching, analyzing, and testing products to recommend the best picks for most consumers.

Source: bestreviews.com

The product categories they analyze are:
- Fashion
- Fashion accessories
- Automobile
- Infant. Child
- Beauty and personal care
- Bath
- Camping and outdoor
- Health and wellness
- Home
- Kitchen
- Garden and pets
- Music
- Services
- Sports and fitness
- Shoes
- Tools
- Toys and games
- Travel

The reviews on this website usually follow the following scheme:
- Description of the main features.
- Pros of the product. Positives.
- Negative considerations. Cons of the article.

At the end of each review he includes metrics from the analysis that lend credibility to his research:

Let's take a look at some examples of the different types of reviews that can be found on bestreviews.com:
- **The best...**
    - The best Nintendo consoles
    - Best sewing machines
    - The best gifts of 2020
- **The 5 best...**
  Type of review based on a description and compare 5 excellent choices of products from a niche:
    - Top 5 **refrigerators**
    - Top 5 **iPhone**
    - Top 5 best **mattresses for cribs**
- **Review type A vs. B,** of the type: "The Republic vs. the Empire". "White vs. Black". In this case, two products or two brands that serve the same purpose are analyzed. For example:
    - Comparison between two brands of treadmills. **Peloton vs. Nordictrack**
      https://bestreviews.com/blog/peloton-vs-nordictrack

The bestreviews blog posts are between **1,000 and 1,500 words** long, with a careful SEO strategy, which allows them to be positioned in the top positions in Google.

5. www.safewise.com

On this website they test and compare security products for home and business, with the aim of enabling their users to make smart and safe purchasing decisions, never better said. Estimated monthly traffic: **1,000,000** visits.

They are honest and unbiased reviews of the full range of home and business security products.

The motto of this website is:

"Buy smart. Live safe."

The website's **content** and affiliate marketing **strategy** is based on:

- Security Buyers' **Guides**
    - The best home security systems.
    - The best tenant-installed home security systems. DYI
    - The best security systems for the home with pets.
    - Top 10 Best Wireless Security Cameras of 2021
- **Reviews** of security brands
    - Vivint Review
    - Frontpoint Review
    - SimpliSafe Review
    - ADT Review
    - Blue by ADT Review
- Brand **comparisons**
    - ADT vs Vivint
      Example:
      https://www.safewise.com/blog/adt-vs-vivint/
    - ADT vs. Frontpoint
    - Frontpoint vs Vivint
    - SimpliSafe vs. Frontpoint
    - SimpliSafe vs. ring
- **They provide** home safety **guides and resources on the blog**, such as:
    - Everything you need to know about home security.
      https://www.safewise.com/everything-you-need-to-know-about-home-security/
    - How much does a home security system cost?
    - How to choose a security system
    - 10 simple ways to protect your new home
    - What to do after a robbery
    - Frequently asked questions about home security

6. wirecutter.com

It is a generalist review website. It covers multiple categories. Average number of monthly visits: **12,000,000**.

Wirecutter helps users find the best products in a wide variety of categories.

Wirecutter (www.nytimes.com/wirecutter) is owned by the New York Times (digital newspaper with an estimated **376 million** visits each month).

NYT, through **wirecutter,** monetizes traffic with affiliate marketing.

Inspiring idea

Follow Wirecutter's email marketing strategy. They send a daily newsletter with offers and information to their subscribers.

Wirecutter has built up a community of loyal followers, who rely on its thoughtful and detailed reviews to make purchasing decisions, and in return, the New York Times receives a commission for brokering each sale. Everybody's happy!

Product categories analyzed in Wirecutter:
- Popular.
  For example, review on "The best non-stick frying pan".
- Home & Garden
- Electronics
- Sleep
- Kitchen
- Accessories
- Gifts
- Open air
- Style
- Travel
- Health and fitness
- Baby and child
- Pets
- Hobbies and crafts
- Software
- Office
- Engine

- Adult
- Money

7. www.gearpatrol.com

Gear Patrol is a shopping guide for men, oriented to the male universe, covering topics such as technology, outdoor, style, accessories, among others. Estimated number of monthly visits to its website: **4,000,000.**

Gear Patrol aims to have the format and style of a men's magazine. **For men only!**

Gear Patrol offers product reviews in the following categories:
- Watches
- Engine
- Food and beverage
- Home
- Style
- Technology
- Outdoor
- Sports

Examples of Gear Patrol reviews:
- The 13 Best New Bourbons and Whiskies of 2021 (so far)
- The best road kits you can buy
- The best snowboards of 2021

Gear Patrol uses the following social networks for its affiliate marketing policy: Twitter, Facebook, Instagram, YouTube and Flipboard.

8. www.revistagq.com

GQ in its origins (1957) was called Gentlemen's Quarterly. It is a monthly American magazine that seeks to provide information to men about fashion, style, and men's culture. Estimated monthly traffic: **5,000,000** visits.

Contains articles on: food, movies, health, sex, music, travel, sports, technology and literature.

GQ is considered more exclusive and sophisticated than other magazines of the same genre, such as Maxim and FHM.

GQ stands out for showing the latest trends in men's fashion, sneakers, series, movies, netflix universe, technology, iphone, amazon, sports and business.

Examples of reviews that can be found in **GQ:**
- The best white sneakers from Nike, adidas, Vans, Reebok, Puma, New Balance...
- The men's sweatshirts you should own because they never go out of style and go with everything
- 7 Eastpak backpacks at discount prices
- 15 gym backpacks that will encourage you to retire yours for good
- 13 sneakers suitable for back to the office

9.- www.younghouselove.com

Home renovation and decoration blog. They provide do-it-yourself, decoration and handicraft **tips.** Estimated monthly traffic: **400,000** visits

Let's take a look at some examples of **content** that users interested in these topics can find on the web:
- Holiday gift guides for everyone.
- Gifts for adults
- How to store everything in a small kitchen
- How to clean a soiled second-hand carpet

10. www.pcworld.es

Pcworld provides information and expert advice on laptops, smartphones, operating systems, headsets, software, web hosting, antivirus, tablets - in short, a wide variety of technology products. Estimated number of monthly visits: **1,000,000**

At PC World you can read tutorials, reviews and product listings with the best tips. Categories collected in PCWorld with reviews:
- Smartphones
- Computers
- Tablets

- Reviews
- Best Products. Wide range of technological products and services
- Tutoriales

Example of content:
- Top 10 Android phones of 2021
- The best phablets or full-size mobiles of 2021
- The best cheap wireless in-ear headphones of 2021
- The best electronic mosquito repellents of 2021

Let's take a look at several examples of content published on PCWorld to take advantage of commercial campaigns throughout the year:
- Mother's Day: Best tech gifts for Mother's Day
- Book Day: Where to buy books online
- Sant Jordi: The best online florists to send flowers on Mother's

From the type of reviews and links, we believe they are associated with the following affiliate programs:
- Amazon Associates
- Fnac
- Macnificos (Apple)
- El Corte Ingles
- PcComponents
- Mediamarkt.

They use a multi-affiliate policy to expand assortment, options and proposals to their community.

11. www.xataka.com

www.xataka.com is a digital publication about gadgets and technology. It analyzes the latest news and trends in mobiles, tablets, computing, smartwatch, technological products in general and current science. Average number of monthly visits: **32.000.000**

Xataka is a Webedia publication aimed at all technology enthusiasts. Xataka is in charge of telling in a rigorous and passionate way the current technological news, and of analyzing in depth the main launches and comparing them with other similar models.

"Launched in 2004, Xataka has become the leading Spanish-language technology publication, creating a community of highly informed, influential and highly participative users. Xataka is passion for a future that has already become a reality."

https://www.xataka.com/quienes-somos

Xataka works with several affiliate programs:
- Amazon
- Media Markt
- PCComponents, among others.

This strategy of being associated with several affiliate programs allows you to offer excellent information in your reviews and give the reader the possibility to choose where to buy.

Examples of **reviews** you can find in **Xataka:**
- Realme 7 Pro, analysis. This experience and features for 300 euros make it difficult for the competition.
- Sonos Roam, analysis: the most economical Sonos speaker is already one of the new benchmarks among Bluetooth models.
- Fitbit Ace 3 review: a simple activity tracker for kids with the touch of Fitbit's app
- Pet technology: 19 feeding, play and monitoring devices for your dog or cat

12. www.headphonesaddict.com

headphonesaddict.com is an affiliate marketing website focused on the **Headphones Microniche**.

They offer users guides and reviews to help them make purchasing decisions. Number of monthly visits: **60,000**

They sort the products analyzed into the following categories:
- Headphones. Overview
- Sports
- Noise cancellation
- Cheap. It offers a list of headphones under $30, $50...
- Wireless
- With cable
- Game

- Headband
- Speakers
- About hearing...

13. www.whathifi.com

whathifi.com offers reviews of hi-fi, home theater and technology products.

They provide tips, news, ideas, guides to simplify the purchase of technology and videos giving relevant information about the products they analyze. Estimated monthly traffic: **8,000,000** visits.

Categories of products promoted on whathifi :
- TVs
- Hi-Fi
- Home Cinema
- Accessories
- Tablets & Smartphones
- Headphones. Headphones
- Laptops
- Streaming
- Digital TV Boxes
- Game consoles
- All-in-one computers

Examples of analysis and reviews:
- The best Bose 2021 speakers
- The best Dolby Atmos sound bars 2021
- Review of Sony WH-1000XM4

14. www.thelabradorsite.com

Blog specialized in the **Labrador Retriever** dog breed. This website is a valuable guide with information on how to buy, raise and train dogs of this breed, from puppyhood to adulthood. Estimated monthly traffic: **1.000.000 visits.**

This is a niche site, for Labrador breed dog owners. They offer reviews of Labrador products in the following categories:
- Necklaces
- Toys

- Beds
- Accessories
- Hygiene and cleaning products
- Food
- Cages and carriers
- Necklaces
- Gifts for lovers of two-legged Labradors (...)

This blog is an excellent example of how to detect and reach a specific, clear and concrete community: "The lovers of this endearing breed".

Example of blog **content:**
- Tips for raising a puppy when you work full time
- Dog training methods: choosing the right way to train your labrador
- Best toys and games for Labradors

15. www.mydogsname.com

It is a niche blog, it is a website dedicated to the first animal domesticated by Homo Sapiens and that since then is his best friend: the **dog.** Number of monthly visits on average: **735.000**

The creator of this blog has built an entire ecosystem around the tool that helps users choose the perfect name for their pet.

In addition, the blog has a store with all the necessary products that a dog owner needs, divided into the following categories:
- Toys
- Wet and dry feeding
- Home
- Training
- Hygiene and cleanliness
- Fashion
- Cages and carriers

The affiliate marketing program that mydogsname.com is affiliated with is **Amazon Associates,** paying them a 6% commission on sales (corresponding rate in the first half of 2021).

Do you love dogs, cats, fish, chinchillas, parakeets? Yes, in this case creating a blog and publishing tips on their care, breeding, hygiene, feeding..., is an excellent way to help, create community, have fun and achieve your financial goals.

16. www.redcanina.es

It is a Spanish website that disseminates useful information to dog lovers.

On this site you can find out, which beaches in Spain allow access with your pet, or which parks you can go to with your canine friend, or accommodations that allow dogs (hotels, apartments, camping ...).

Average monthly traffic: 833,000 visits to the site

In short, it provides useful information. There is a lot of information and tips for traveling with your dog, its care, breeding and training. On the page dedicated to the store there is a variety of products for dogs, with reviews, tips and the typical... "The best ....", seeking to convey useful information and facilitate the purchase decision.

Allow me to insist...
Around something we love, in this case our 4-legged pet, we can create a business model based on affiliate marketing.
Cats are your thing? Well, a cat blog...
If in your case you are not into pets and you are into sports...
How about a blog with useful information for those who practice your favorite sport?
Blog about what you love and monetize...€€€€€

---

17. Did someone talk about cats?.... www.para-gatos.net

Spanish blog specialized in the world of cats. Offers advice on health, care, feeding and breeding. Estimated monthly traffic: **100,000** visits

... Hey, that's a lot of miaus :)

Categories with product reviews that you will find on this website:
- Feeding
- Hygiene and health
- Toys
- Home Accessories
- Sandbox
- Beds
- Feeder and Drinker
- Scrapers
- Travel and sightseeing

Example of content:
- Which cat toy to buy? Best cat toy for quality and price
- What is the best shampoo for cats?
- Vitamins and food supplements for cats

This is another excellent example of converting illusion, affection and leisure into business, of transforming the passion for cats into a profitable venture based on affiliate marketing.

Monetize by leveraging your passions

18. www.juguetesparapajaros.com

This website is an example of **Micronicho:** toys for birds.

Its creator struggles to get a share of the traffic from the approximately 15,000 to 20,000 monthly searches for "bird toys" among all Spanish-speaking countries.

This blog monetizes through **Amazon Associates** commissions. Estimated average monthly visits traffic: **750**

Remember that Amazon pays its affiliates for the sale of products in the "pets" category, a 6% commission (2021).

There are other affiliate programs that pay a higher commission percentage, such as https://www.zoobio.es/page/affiliates which pays 10%.

Analyze this program, study if it interests you as an alternative to Amazon's affiliate program or you can partner and work with both affiliate programs. It's up to you.

Example of **content** of this blog:
- **Comparison of the best toys for lovebirds.**

19. www.preparadoparaelfin.com

Blog dedicated to all people concerned about survival in catastrophic situations. This site provides advice and reviews on: survival accessories for the mountains, camping, heavy snowfalls..., or how to face the End of the World. Estimated average number of visits per month: **10,000**.

The blog features a variety of articles to help you survive critical survival situations.

This is an excellent website for users worried about the day of the end of the world (let's hope it won't come soon...), but also for all those who love nature and outdoor adventures.

Example of **content:**
- How to be prepared for a global epidemic or pandemic
- The best tactical fanny packs in military style
- The best ballistic, tactical and sunglasses to protect you from the sun

20. www.equipamientotactico.net

Blog for lovers of uniforms and the military world, if you want or need to dress like a military, police or have the necessary equipment to enjoy your Airsoft battles, this is your website.

Estimated average monthly visits: **40,000**

This blog is a simple product listing, with hardly any reviews or tips. It is about listing products and positioning with a good SEO strategy.

It gets 14,000 visits, not bad for lacking "brainy" contributions. Product categories collected on the web:
- Security guard
- Police Equipment
- Clothing
- Accessories

- Self-defense

Store categories:
- Police Equipment and Material
- Safety equipment
- Security guard equipment
- Military and tactical boots
- Tactical Flashlights
- Survival kits
- Military and tactical knives
- Military jackets. Tactical jackets
- Military sleeping bags
- Tactical gloves for military, police, army, navy seals
- Emergency rations
- Tactical belts
- Military tactical pants
- Books with tactical and military techniques
- Tactical combat backpacks
- Key ring with personal alarm
- Military tactical wallets
- Military Watches
- Tactical Pens
- Camouflage Paint
- Tactical Vests
- Tactical T-shirts
- Blank Pistols
- Buy Anti-Cut Sleeves
- Extendable Batons
- Anti-Theft Wallets
- Hydration backpacks
- Military Patches
- Headlamps
- Military rangefinders
- Tactical fanny packs
- Anti-cut gloves
- Military combat compasses
- Police goggles
- Military balaclavas
- Technical Socks
- Combat bags

- Chemical lights
- Military canteens
- Military caps and berets
- Survival knives
- Energy bars
- Military boots
- Anti-theft backpacks
- Military backpacks
- Camouflage nets
- Tactical goggles
- Ballistic Glasses
- Portable stoves
- Water purification tablets
- Handheld GPS
- Survival bracelets
- Walkie talkies
- Gas masks
- Military tents
- Night vision goggles

21. www.blogcamping.com (Chronicles of a first-time camper)
This is a personal blog that includes information about:
- Travel chronicles
- Information for campers
- Tips to follow if you buy a caravan
- Ideas and do-it-yourself tricks to have our caravan ready for use.
- Care and maintenance of caravans, motorhomes or camper vans.
- Recommendations for campers
- Kitchen for campers
- (...)

Estimated number of monthly visits: **8,500**.

22. www.todocamping.es
Web with information for campers and hikers.

It also deals with survival and outdoor issues. Estimated number of visits per month: 1,500. This blog is specialized in all kinds of camping equipment: tents, camping furniture, kitchen equipment and much more.

The categories of products listed in the todocamping.es store:
- Tents
- Sleeping bags
- Kitchen
- Furniture
- Accessories
- Caravans

The todocamping blog is a compilation of tips for campers with affiliate links to drive traffic to Amazon:

Examples of reviews and tips what we can find in todocamping:
- 10 most useful and best-selling accessories for your caravan
- Tips for teleworking in a caravan
- The best products for the care of a caravan
- The best GPS for caravan travel
- 5 tips to avoid the heat in a caravan
- The best products and tips for safe sleeping in a caravan
- The 8 must-have accessories to turn your van into a camper van
- The best products for cooking in a caravan
- The best bike racks for camping

This website has a defect that should be corrected by the administrator. The price indicated on the website does not always match the price listed on Amazon, this causes bad image of the blog.

Key idea

Dear reader, showing different prices on your website and on Amazon is unprofessional, it detracts from the credibility of your site, your advice and your reviews. Avoid it, don't let it happen on your blog. It looks terrible.

---

23. www.guitarra-acustica.com

Blog created for the community of music lovers, acoustic and classical guitar. Estimated number of monthly visits: **15.000.**

The primary objective of this website is to teach acoustic guitar playing. The blog guitarra-acustica.com shares content of all kinds:
- Lessons
- Scores
- Tabs
- Purchasing tips
- Buying guides
- How to tune the guitar
- Analysis of the different models of acoustic guitars
- Videos
- Interviews
- Reports

24. www.7mejor.top

Online shopping guide and comparison site. Estimated number of monthly visits: **140,000.** Provides information on the following categories:
- Sports
- Electric bicycles
- Heart rate monitors
- Sports watches
- Trail running shoes
- Electronics
- Leisure
- Home
- Kitchen
- (...)

In the description of each product they always use the same scheme, it is divided into three sections:
1. Product description
2. Advantages
3. Inconveniences

Key idea

This division into three sections is excellent; it is a winning structure, both in terms of design and in terms of attractiveness and clarity.

It also helps and improves SEO positioning. Keep this in mind for your strategy as a marketer.

The name of the domain **7mejor.top is a** declaration of intentions about the content that you will find on this website.

In general, for each category reviewed, they lIst a ranking of the best purchase options. It lists from worst to best, from position 7 to 1. For example:
- The Best Electric Bicycles of 2021 - Guide and Comparison
- Top 7 proteins of 2021

There are rankings and analyses that start from position 10 instead of 7. A comparative with more products has more options to position, more options to attract traffic and more conversion options. For example:
- Top 10 best bluetooth headsets of 2021
- Top 10 board games of 2021

They monetize by directing traffic to **Amazon** and collecting commissions on each sale brokered.

This website, both for traffic, cleanliness, simplicity of design and content, is an excellent affiliate marketing website model that you should take into account.

He is a worthy reference and example that you should take into account.

On the 7mejor.top website they do not publish the prices, they only indicate on the button: **SEE PRICE** and redirect to the Amazon website where the user will see the amount of the product and the rest of the information.

25. www.accesoriospatineteelectrico.com

Blog with information about electric scooters, E-Bikes and Accessories. Provides comparisons and news of these products. Estimated number of monthly visits: **85,000**.

Let's take a look at some examples of the type of **content** that this website offers to users of scooters and electric bicycles:

Type listed:
- Top 10 best electric scooters of 2021: Comparison and guide
- Top 10 best electric scooters of 2021: Comparison and guide
- The 5 best Xiaomi electric scooters of 2021: Comparison
- The 5 best Xiaomi electric scooters of 2021: Comparison
- The 8 best Cecotec electric scooters of 2021: Comparison
- The 8 best Cecotec electric scooters of 2021: Comparison
- The 7 best electric scooter helmets of 2021: Comparison and guide

Comparison:
- Scooters Cecotec Bongo vs Xiaomi Mi Electric Scooter: Which one is better? Comparison 2021

Top:
- The TOP Electric Scooters of this year 2021
- Cecotec Bongo A-Series scooter review: Reviews of the best value for money scooter
- Cecotec Bongo A-Series scooter review: Reviews of the best value for money scooter

This website collaborates with several affiliate programs:
- Amazon affiliates
- storececotec.com
- alltricks.com

$ $ $ $ $

25 turnover estimates. The results will fill you with optimism

We have seen 25 excellent websites that monetize with affiliate marketing. We ask ourselves, what is their earning potential? We don't know their exact profits, but we can work out different hypotheses, contemplate different scenarios. Let's get down to it:

Hypothesis we make:
- Estimated conversion rate: 3%.
- What monthly earnings could be obtained with a commission per sale of: **5€, 20€, 30€, 50€.**
- **Traffic.** We use for the calculations the one indicated above in the description given.

NO.	WEB	Monthly earnings assumptions	
		5 €	20 €
1	dealnews.com	1.050.000 €	4.200.000 €
2	thisiswhyimbroke.com	150.000 €	600.000 €
3	buzzfeed.com	18.750.000 €	75.000.000 €
4	bestreviews.com	1.050.000 €	4.200.000 €
5	safewise.com	150.000 €	600.000 €
6	nytimes.com/wirecutter	1.800.000 €	7.200.000 €
7	gearpatrol.com	600.000 €	2.400.000 €
8	revistagq.com	750.000 €	3.000.000 €
9	bluetooth-headphones	4.950 €	19.800 €
10	pcworld.com	150.000 €	600.000 €
11	xataka.com	4.800.000 €	19.200.000 €
12	headphonesaddict.com	9.000 €	36.000 €
13	whathifi.com/us	1.200.000 €	4.800.000 €
14	thelabradorsite.com	150.000 €	600.000 €

15	mydogsname.com	110.250 €	441.000 €
16	redcanina.es	124.950 €	499.800 €
17	for-cats.net	15.000 €	60.000 €
18	toysforbirds	113 €	450 €
19	preparateparaelfin.com	1500 €	6000 €
20	equipamientotactico.net	6.000 €	24.000 €
21	blogcamping.com	1.275 €	5.100 €
22	todocamping.es	225 €	900 €
23	guitarra-acustica.com	2.250 €	9.000 €
24	7best.top	21.000 €	84.000 €
25	accessorieselectr.scooter	12.750 €	51.000 €

NO.	WEB	Monthly earnings assumptions	
		30 €	50 €
1	dealnews.com/	6.300.000 €	10.500.000 €
2	thisiswhyimbroke.com/	900.000 €	1.500.000 €
3	buzzfeed.com/	112.500.000 €	187.500.000 €
4	bestreviews.com/	6.300.000 €	10.500.000 €
5	safewise.com/	900.000 €	1.500.000 €
6	nytimes.com/wirecutter/	10.800.000 €	18.000.000 €
7	gearpatrol.com/	3.600.000 €	6.000.000 €
8	revistagq.com/	4.500.000 €	7.500.000 €
9	bluetooth-headphon	29.700 €	49.500 €

	es.com/		
10	pcworld.com/	900.000 €	1.500.000 €
11	xataka.com/	28.800.000 €	48.000.000 €
12	headphonesaddict.com/	54.000 €	90.000 €
13	whathifi.com/us	7.200.000 €	12.000.000 €
14	thelabradorsite.com/	900.000 €	1.500.000 €
15	mydogsname.com/	661.500 €	1.102.500 €
16	redcanina.es/	749.700 €	1.249.500 €
17	para-gatos.net/	90.000 €	150.000 €
18	toysforbirds.com/	675 €	1.125 €
19	preparateparaelfin.com/	900 €	1.500 €
20	equipamientotactico.net/	12.600 €	21.000 €
21	blogcamping.com/	7.650 €	12.750 €
22	todocamping.es/	1.350 €	2.250 €
23	guitarra-acustica.com/	13.500 €	22.500 €
24	7best.top/	126.000 €	210.000 €
25	accessoriesskateboardelect.	76.500 €	127.500 €

The following tables are ordered according to the estimated monthly traffic, in the first positions the websites with less traffic.

NO.	WEB	Monthly earnings assumptions	
		5 €	20 €
1	toysforbirds.com/	113 €	450 €
2	preparateparaelfin.com/	150 €	600 €
3	todocamping.es/	225 €	900 €
4	blogcamping.com/	1.275 €	5.100 €
5	equipamientotactico.net/	2.100 €	8.400 €
6	guitarra-acustica.com/	2.250 €	9.000 €
7	bluetooth-headphones.	4.950 €	19.800 €
8	headphonesaddict.com/	9.000 €	36.000 €
9	accesoriospatineteelectri	12.750 €	51.000 €
10	para-gatos.net/	15.000 €	60.000 €
11	7best.top/	21.000 €	84.000 €
12	mydogsname.com/	110.250 €	441.000 €
13	redcanina.es/	124.950 €	499.800 €
14	.thisiswhyimbroke.com	150.000 €	600.000 €
15	safewise.com/	150.000 €	600.000 €
16	pcworld.com/	150.000 €	600.000 €
17	thelabradorsite.com/	150.000 €	600.000 €
18	gearpatrol.com/	600.000 €	2.400.000 €
19	revistagq.com/	750.000 €	3.000.000 €
20	dealnews.com/	1.050.000 €	4.200.000 €
21	bestreviews.com/	1.050.000 €	4.200.000 €
22	whathifi.com/us	1.200.000 €	4.800.000 €
23	nytimes.com/wirecutter/	1.800.000 €	7.200.000 €

24	xataka.com/	4.800.000 €	19.200.000 €
25	buzzfeed.com/	18.750.000 €	75.000.000 €

NO.	WEB	Monthly earnings assumptions	
		30 €	50 €
1	toysforbirds.com	675 €	1.125 €
2	preparateparaelfin.co	9.000 €	15.000 €
3	todocamping.es	1.350 €	2.250 €
4	blogcamping.com	7.650 €	12.750 €
5	equipamientotactico.	36.000 €	60.000 €
6	guitarra-acustica.com	13.500 €	22.500 €
7	bluetooth-headphones	29.700 €	49.500 €
8	headphonesaddict.co	54.000 €	90.000 €
9	accessories scooter	76.500 €	127.500 €
10	for-cats.net	90.000 €	150.000 €
11	7best.top	126.000 €	210.000 €
12	mydogsname.com	661.500 €	1.102.500 €
13	redcanina.es	749.700 €	1.249.500 €
14	thisiswhyimbroke.com	900.000 €	1.500.000 €
15	safewise.com	900.000 €	1.500.000 €
16	pcworld.com	900.000 €	1.500.000 €
17	thelabradorsite.com	900.000 €	1.500.000 €
18	gearpatrol.com	3.600.000 €	6.000.000 €
19	revistagq.com	4.500.000 €	7.500.000 €
20	dealnews.com	6.300.000 €	10.500.000 €
21	bestreviews.com	6.300.000 €	10.500.000 €
22	whathifi.com	7.200.000 €	12.000.000 €

23	nytimes.com/wire	10.800.000 €	18.000.000 €
24	xataka.com	28.800.000 €	48.000.000 €
25	buzzfeed.com	112.500.000 €	187.500.000 €

Depending on the traffic, the commission we get for each promoted sale and the conversion rate, we will obtain one or another income figure. Obtaining significant income depends on the traffic, its quality, the choice of the affiliate program and the products that we are going to promote. It only depends on you, on your effort and perseverance.

With little traffic is it possible to have a significant income? Yes, if one or more of the following hypotheses apply:
1. We obtain a **high commission** from each promoted sale.
2. **We increase** the "Conversion Rate". In the previous hypothesis we have estimated that 3% of the traffic to your website ends up buying on the merchant's website, if we improve this percentage we will need less traffic to achieve our financial goals. Aliexpress boasts conversion rates above 30%.
3. Both. The sum of the two previous hypotheses. We get **more profit** per sale and achieve **higher conversion rates.**

Let's see an example, we create a blog to provide tips to newbies in wordpress: crackswp.com. We get the following metrics:
- 5,000 visits per month
- 5% conversion
- **40€** commission per sale (hosting + domain...)
  Monthly profit = 10.000€.
  Annual turnover = 120.000€.
  How did we do the calculations?
  5,000 visits x 0.05 conversion x 40€/commission = 10,000€/month
  10,000 x 12 months = 120,000 per annum
- Working with affiliate programs with commissions of 50, 75 or 100€ the income skyrockets to 150K, 225K and 300K€ (in Hotmart you have a lot of digital products with high commissions).

Long live affiliate marketing!

Estimated conversion   5,00%

WEB	Visits per month	Monthly earnings assumptions		
		15 €	25 €	40 €
crackswp.com	5.000	3.750 €	6.250 €	10.000 €
	Annual profit:	45.000 €	75.000 €	120.000 €

Estimated conversion   5,00%

WEB	Visits per month	Monthly earnings assumptions		
		50 €	75 €	100 €
crackswp.com	5.000	12.500 €	18.750 €	25.000 €
	Annual profit:	150.000 €	225.000 €	300.000 €

$ $ $ $ $

How to do affiliate marketing on social networks

In this chapter we are going to look at how to use social networks to promote our affiliate links and earn commissions. Let's look at the different promotion strategies we can adopt on social networks:

Instagram:
- Publish stories inserting affiliate links, sharing content such as: advantages and disadvantages of the product.
- Use quality photos.

Facebook
- Share content including your affiliate links, from your personal or business account.
- Participate in Facebook groups in your niche or category.
- Create your own group. Get to lead your own community on Facebook

YouTube
How are you on camera? Good? Do you like it? Yeah? Ready and action. Take 1. Quiet. Let's roll.
- Record videos that include quality content, with useful information for your community. Example of relevant content for your users that generate traffic to the merchant's website, conversions and commissions:
    1.- Create tutorials .
    2.- Record product videos with reviews, unboxing, comparisons.
    3.- Share type listings:
        - The 5 best microphones for youtubers...
        - The 5 best portable coolers...
        - The 5 best 5G mid-range cell phones...
- Insert your affiliate links in the video description. Remember to be honest and sincere at all times.

Remember that success in affiliate marketing is based on creating long-term bonds with your community.

X-Twitter

Twitter is also another excellent social network for your affiliate marketing strategy. You can:
- Provide information about the products you promote, listings, comparisons.
- Disseminate relevant niche content
- Selling products

Key ideas

Remember to include in all your social media posts a link that leads to the landing page so that the user can sign up to your mailing list.

Offer in exchange for the email address something free (ebook, participate in a sweepstakes, webinar...). The more valuable the gift is perceived to be, the higher your email harvest will be.

Your subscriber list is an important source of income.

$ $ $ $ $

Part 7. The Road

The treasure trail to a monthly turnover of 10,000 €. Step by step guide. Checklist

This chapter is the **step-by-step guide** you need to follow to succeed, succeed and earn more than **10.000 € every month**, thanks to affiliate marketing.

Follow this route, it is an outline of everything you have to do, the steps you have to follow, what you have to do and how. Work hard, persevere and you will succeed. Sure, without a doubt.

Time to act. Get to it. The itinerary I propose is as follows:

1.- Know yourself. Look inside yourself:
- What do you like?
- What activities do you enjoy?
- What do you enjoy?
- List 10 activities you enjoy

2.- Establish financial objectives.
- Decide your financial plan. Income and expenses
- Set monthly turnover targets.
- Decide on the set of actions you must undertake to meet the revenue budget.
- In a spreadsheet create a timing, a calendar with objectives, actions, compliance dates, set objectives. **Set goals and quantify.**

3.- Be creative. Do it differently. Do not do more of the same. Use creativity techniques, such as:
- What if...?
- Brainstorming (brainstorming)
- Dream, let your imagination fly

4.- Niche research
- Do keyword analysis of the niches you want to investigate

- Choose a niche. Decide which one you are going to work with

5.- Select an affiliate program and products. Investigate the following aspects of each program:
- Commission rate
- Conversion rate
- Duration of cookies
- Financial solvency of the merchant
- Reputation
- Customer Service
- Choose to work with programs that report recurring income. Month to month

6.- Choose which products you are going to promote. Study:
- Expected yield
- Conversion rate
- Whenever possible, select products with recurring income or consumption.
- Make a list of 10 products that you are going to start promoting.

7.- Create your blog in wordpress. You need:
- Domain
- Hosting
- Installing your WordPress blog on the hosting
- Select a free template
- Create the design and appearance of the blog
- Install and configure extensions (plugins)

8.- Write valuable and unique content.
- Research on **Quora** what issues your community is concerned about.
- For inspiration, surf the Internet, visit blogs that deal with topics similar to yours.
- What gets the most interactions on social networks, ask your community what topics they would like to see you blog about...
- Write useful, problem-solving posts that can only be found on your blog.

- Be different. Be different, either by what you say or how you say it.
- Create a publication calendar, make it public and respect it.

9.- Insert your affiliate links in the unique and valuable content you have generated.

10.- Develop the strategy to build your subscriber list and do email marketing.
- Decide which plugins to install in your WordPress that make this task easier for you.
- Subscribe to an email marketing tool that could simplify all the necessary actions (autoresponders, segmentation, automate newsletter sending, create sales funnels...).

11.- Implement strategies to **get traffic to your blog.** Remember to review the 15 options are:
- Create valuable content. Post published on your blog with relevant information for the community that follows you, this is what we call Content Marketing or Inbound Marketing.
- Do SEO. Apply organic positioning strategies so that your valuable content appears in the first positions in Google.
- Write as a guest on blogs with a similar theme to yours
- Leave comments on related blogs
- Share the content on your Social Networks
- Include your blog address in all your email signatures.
- Email marketing. Create your subscriber list and transform your audience into a community.
- Answer questions on Quora
- Record and broadcast videos on YouTube. In the description of each video include your blog domain and the links to the promoted products.
- Live webinars, advertise your blog.
- Social networks. Facebook, Instagram, Twitter..., in every post you share on social networks include your affiliate links.
- Instant messaging platform such as whatsapp or telegram

- Include the blog address and affiliate links in the content you create in eBook format, or in PDF, in power point presentation (...)
- Maybe from a podcast...
- Participating in forums, Contribute valuable content and include your affiliate links.

12.- Analyze the data in Google Analytics.
Research:
- Traffic to your website
- Demographics of the traffic to your website
- Most viewed pages
- Conversion rate
- Promoted products that convert the most

13.- Test. Make a mistake.
Correct and learn from mistakes. Make mistakes less and less and better.

14.- Improve your skills.
Practice continuous improvement. Develop a training plan aimed at developing your hard and soft skills.

15.- Make it scalable.
When you have mastered all phases of affiliate marketing and have achieved success with your first affiliate blog. Replicate your system. Create more blogs related to more topics that pique your interest. Keep growing.

Entrepreneur friend, act, **take action, start now, right now**, lay the foundations to conquer your **financial peace of mind**. This will come when your income equals your expenses.

"When you hesitate to act, always choose to do or not to do.
If you make a mistake you will at least have the experience."
Alejandro Jodorowsky

$ $ $ $ $

Hi, I'm Jack

This book it's about how to help you quickly earn €10,000 a month through affiliate marketing or much more.

However, I didn't want to end without a brief comment about me. You know me as **Jack S. Hood**. I'm a manager who has worked in large corporations, I have international and entrepreneurial experience.

An inveterate reader, dreamer, collector of experiences and mentor (at least I try) of restless souls who seek to improve day by day as people and professionals.

Affiliate marketing done. An easy beginner's guide to the secrets of affiliate marketing, it is a manual for you to master the art of making money online and become independent from the stupid little bosses and find your professional path in a fun and easy way.

If you liked this manual, it would be great if you could give an honest and sincere review of the book on the Amazon website. Thank you for your time!

Good luck on the road. On your way. I hope you enjoyed the reading and it is useful for your purposes.

A big hug. Jack

"Fate mixes up the cards.
We play them."

Arthur Schopenhauer

www.ingramcontent.com/pod-product-compliance
Lightning Source LLC
Chambersburg PA
CBHW070244230526
45470CB00002B/479